国 家 文 物 局

主 编

中 国

重要考古发现

文物出版社

2005 · 5

图书在版编目(CIP)数据

2004 中国重要考古发现／国家文物局编．－北京：
文物出版社，2005.5
ISBN 7-5010-1741-7

Ⅰ.2… Ⅱ.国… Ⅲ.考古发现－中国－2004
Ⅳ.K87

中国版本图书馆 CIP 数据核字(2005)第 040392 号

2004 中国重要考古发现

国家文物局 主编

文物出版社出版发行
北京五四大街 29 号
http://www.wenwu.com
E-mail web@wenwu.com
北京圣彩虹制版印刷技术有限公司印刷
2005 年 5 月第一版　2005 年 5 月第一次印制
787 × 1092　1/16　印张：12
ISBN 7-5010-1741-7/K·914
定价：80 元

State Administration of
Cultural Heritage

MAJOR ARCHAEOLOGICAL
DISCOVERIES IN

Cultural Relics Publishing House

Beijing 2005

编辑委员会

协作单位

中国社会科学院考古研究所
北京市文物研究所
天津市文化遗产保护中心
河北省文物研究所
山西省考古研究所
南京博物院
浙江省文物考古研究所
安徽省文物考古研究所
江西省文物考古研究所
山东省文物考古研究所
河南省文物考古研究所
湖北省文物考古研究所
湖南省文物考古研究所
四川省文物考古研究院
陕西省考古研究所
甘肃省文物考古研究所
新疆文物考古研究所
北京大学考古文博学院
山东大学东方考古研究中心
四川大学历史文化学院考古系
西北大学文博学院考古系
南京市博物馆
扬州市文物局
杭州市文物研究所
聊城市文物局
青州市文物局
长沙简牍博物馆
长沙市文物考古研究所
西安市文物保护考古所
吐鲁番地区文物局
《文物》编辑部

主要撰稿人

武仙竹	陈明慧	屈胜明	孙国平	黄渭金
段宏振	李新伟	马萧林	薛新明	王炜林
马明志	梁中合	贾笑冰	徐新民	楼 航
杨根文	蒋卫东	陈 云	方燕明	王 辉
赵丛苍	许 宏	赵海涛	李志鹏	陈国梁
郁金城	郭京宁	王京燕	谢尧亭	马 升
田建文	向桃初	王 峰	胡常春	郑同修
王瑞霞	庄明军	周科华	王 芬	栾丰实
吕恩国	张永兵	宋少华	金 平	毛瑞林
刘振东	张建锋	孙福喜	程林泉	张翔宇
田亚岐	王 颢	景宏伟	盛立双	安家瑶
龚国强	何岁利	李春林	李永宪	霍 巍
李荣华	赖祖龙	余盛华	汪 勃	刘 涛
印志华	池 军	郭木森	吴顺东	朱岩石
何利群	王志高	马 涛	贾维勇	华国荣
祁海宁	骆 鹏			

目 录 CONTENTS

目 录 CONTENTS

前 言 PREFACE

　　2004年的田野考古工作可谓硕果累累，众多的考古发现以其发掘的科学性、资料的珍贵性带给人们一次又一次的惊喜。我局从批准的调查、勘探、发掘项目中遴选出本年度具有代表性和重要学术价值的37项考古发现，编辑了《2004中国重要考古发现》。

　　在湖北郧西黄龙洞遗址发现5枚晚期智人牙齿化石，同时出土有文化遗物和大量伴生动物群化石，为研究晚期智人提供了重要资料。浙江余姚田螺山遗址是继河姆渡、鲻山遗址之后，河姆渡文化早期遗存的又一次重要发现。平湖庄桥坟良渚文化墓地发掘清理中晚期墓葬236座，出土各类随葬品近2600件(组)，是迄今发现的规模最大的良渚文化墓地。在陕西吴堡后寨子峁遗址发现70余座房址和保存完好的石围墙，有可能代表该地区一种新的考古学文化类型。

　　甘肃酒泉西河滩遗址是一处较大规模的新石器晚期至青铜时代聚落遗址，在此发现大量房址、窖穴、窑址、墓葬，出土一批陶、玉、骨、铜器等。河南偃师二里头遗址发现的宫城城墙是迄今可确认的我国最早的宫城遗迹，另外还发现了车辙、大型夯土基址、绿松石器制造作坊等。在山西柳林高红商代遗址发现的大面积夯土基址以及浮山桥北晚商墓地发现的多座大型墓葬，对研究山西地区夏商时期的文化面貌具有重要意义。在湖南宁乡炭河里遗址发现商周时期的城址和大型人工土台建筑，以及数座贵族墓葬，出土了大量青铜器和玉器。有迹象表明，该城址与备受关注的宁乡商周青铜器群有着密切联系。

　　湖南长沙走马楼8号古井发现万余枚墨书西汉简牍，内容多是当时的行政司法文书，是继走马楼三国吴简之后的又一次重大发现。甘肃成县尖川西汉墓地的发掘、陕西西安汉长安城长乐宫四号建筑基址、凤翔西汉汧河码头仓储建筑遗址、西安理工大学西汉壁画墓、天津蓟县小毛庄东汉画像石墓等，为汉代考古研究提供了重要资料。

　　继安伽墓和史君墓之后，在西安北郊又发现一座北周粟特人墓葬(康业墓)，出土一具完整的围屏石榻，线雕精美，内容丰富。该墓的发掘为研究北朝时期在华粟特人的生活、丧葬习俗以及中西文化交流，尤其为研究中国古代绘画史提供了珍贵资料。中日联合考古队对唐长安城大明宫遗址内的太液池、蓬莱岛进行发掘，发现多处园林建筑遗迹，是研究唐代皇家园林的重要资料。

　　扬州唐城考古队对宋大城北门水门遗址进行的抢救性发掘，证明了文献中关于宋大城有水门的记载以及《营造法式》中的有关记述。杭州南宋临安城考古工作取得新进展，通过调查、勘探、试掘，基本确定了临安城皇城的范围和中心宫殿区的布局。

　　边疆地区考古工作2004年也取得重要收获。新疆鄯善洋海墓地几年来累计发掘509座墓葬，出土器物非常丰富，有陶、木、青铜、石、铁、骨、角器以及皮革制品、毛织物等。其年代为公元前1000年至公元前后，是研究这一地区青铜时代文化以及文化交流的重要资料。四川大学考古系等单位在西藏阿里地区象泉河上游进行考古调查，发现多处古代遗址，其中尤以象雄时代的"琼隆银城"遗址最为引人注目。

　　2004年，国家文物局审查批准重要考古发掘项目600余项，涵盖了史前至明清的各个时段，其中大多数为配合基本建设工程的抢救性发掘项目。广大考古工作者怀着强烈的使命感、责任感，将课题意识和学术思想融入到配合基本建设的考古工作中，取得世人瞩目的成绩。可以说，每一项发现都凝聚着考古人的汗水和心血。谨以此册快报向那些栉风沐雨、常年奔波在考古第一线的同志们表示敬意！

湖北黄龙洞
晚期智人遗址

SITE OF LATE HOMO SAPIENS
IN THE HUANGLONG CAVE, HUBEI

黄龙洞位于湖北省郧西县香口镇李师关村,为大型管状溶洞。洞穴处于秦岭东段南坡的丘陵山地,发育于古生界寒武系灰岩。洞口的原始宽度约27.8、高约11米。现已初步探明,洞穴水平深度约400余米(未到底)。洞口面向东北,北纬33°07′,东经110°13′,海拔约598米。洞口前有发源于秦岭的大水河(汉江支流),洞口高出河水约8米。洞穴后部是绵延的黄龙山,主峰1277米,洞口前是顺着大水河发育的绵延平川。洞内的堆积物深

厚,洞穴原始堆积物与洞穴顶部的间距不大。

2004年6~12月,湖北省文物考古研究所对黄龙洞进行了考古发掘。发现5枚晚期智人牙齿化石,同时出土了文化遗物和大量的伴生动物群化石。

黄龙洞发掘区的主剖面从上至下有6层。第1层,顶钙板层(洞穴化学沉积物),厚约2~28厘米。第2层,砂砾层,厚26~201厘米。第3层,红色粉砂质黏土层,厚28~43厘米。层内发育有钙板。

黄龙洞远景
A distant view of the
Huanglong Cave

2

黄龙洞发掘现场
Site of excavation in the Huanglong Cave

考古发掘现场
Site of archaeological excavation

在洞内深处，该层包含有哺乳动物化石。第4层，棕红色粉砂质黏土层，厚32～68厘米。夹杂石灰岩角砾等。该层在洞内出土人化石和哺乳动物化石。第5层，石灰岩风化物堆积层，厚41～66厘米。结构较松散，主要为石灰岩风化角砾等。第6层，红色粉砂质黏土层，厚18～26厘米。结构较紧密，无包含物。以下为基岩(寒武系灰岩)。上述各地层中，第5、6层在出土人化石、文化遗物的YHNI区尚未挖掘到底。

发掘出土的5枚人牙化石，分别为左上第二门齿、左上犬齿、左上第三白齿、左下第三白齿、右下第二白齿。有两枚磨耗较轻，另3枚磨耗较重。从年龄特征和齿序位置分析，它们可能分属于不同个体。牙齿化石都保存得比较好，齿冠、齿根等部分特征清淅。5枚人牙化石的主要特征，还显示了

从"北京人"至现代中国人之间演化特征上的连续性。例如从形态上观察，上外侧门齿具有典型的铲形结构。从测量数据上考察，齿冠面积尺寸位于中早期智人与晚期智人之间，偏向于晚期智人。

遗址中文化遗物包括石制品和骨制品。石制品主要为使用器具类，可分石锤、手镐、尖刃器、砍砸器、刮削器、使用石片等。原料包括碧玉岩、石英岩、流纹岩、燧石、砂岩等，器型有大有小。石器加工一般比较细致，刃形较为规整。骨制品也主要为使用性器物，均用硬锤打制而成。器型较大，刃形比较规则，包括尖刃类和宽刃类两种。

和古人类牙齿化石同层出土的动物化石种类较多，经初步鉴定，主要有猕猴、螃蟹、印度假吸血蝠、刺猬、豪猪、竹鼠、鬣狗、豺、狼、果子狸、大熊猫、黑熊、华南虎、东方剑齿象、中国犀、华

南巨貘、野猪、梅花鹿、羚羊等 30 多种，数量逾 1200 余件，动物群的基本特征，表现出我国南方大熊猫—剑齿象动物群的特点。其中有些小型动物化石种类(如印度假吸血蝠)，可能是在大熊猫—剑齿象动物群中首次出现。

遗址中没有发现石器制作过程中的备料、废弃品或碎屑片等。并且人类化石、动物化石、文化遗物等均集中分布于洞穴深处的 YHNI 区，距洞口约 140 米。这里可能是当时古人类活动的中心区域。

根据遗址中心区域所在位置、文化遗物以及洞口朝向、洞穴形态、洞口附近冬季气候特点等推测，黄龙洞古人类遗址或许是一个季节性遗址。

黄龙洞遗址古人类牙齿化石与中国现代人关系比较紧密，属晚期智人。黄龙洞古人类遗址应属于晚更新世，铀系法测年校正结果为距今 94000 年。这是中国和东亚迄今所知最早的晚期智人遗址，它填补了东亚早期智人向晚期智人演化的缺环，对研究中国和东亚现代人的来源等具有重要意义。

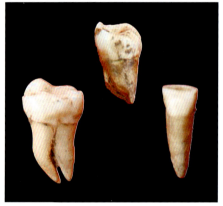

晚期智人牙齿化石
Fossil teeth of late *Homo sapiens*

石手镐
Stone hand-pick

石砍砸器
Stone chopping tool

The Huanglong Cave is a large-sized tube-shaped limestone grotto. It was developed from the limestone of the Cambrian Period in the hills of the southern slope of the eastern Qinling Mountains, at the present-day Xiangkou Town, Yunxi County. Its mouth was originally about 27.8 m wide and some 11 m high, and approximately 400 m in horizontal depth according to preliminary exploration (not reaching the end). The entrance is about 598 m above the sea level, faces to the northeast, and lies by the Dashui River rising in the Qinling Mountains, a tributary of the Hanjiang River, at about 8 m height above the river water. Behind the cave stretches Mt. Huanglong with the main peak 1277 m high; and in front of it a plain spreads along the Dashui River.

In June − December 2004, the Hubei Provincial Institute of Cultural Relics and Archaeology discovered five fossil teeth of late *Homo sapiens* in the cave, at a depth of about 140 m, in association with cultural relics and quantities of faunal fossils. The human teeth are the left second incisor, canine and third molar of upper jaw, and right second molar and left third molar of mandible. All of them are rather good in condition, with clear features of the crown and root.

The cultural relics fall into stone and bone artifacts. The former group includes hand-picks, chopping tools, scrapers and used flakes; the latter, large-sized pointed- and wide-edged tools. The associated faunal fossils are rich in variety. According to preliminary identification, there are the macaque, crab, hedgehog, porcupine, bamboo rat, hyena, giant panda, cave bear, tiger, stegodon, rhinoceros, South China tapir, etc., altogether more than 30 specimens, numbering above 1,200 pieces. They show features of South China giant panda-stegodon fauna. The calibrated data of a uranium-series dating suggest the site to go back 94,000 BP. This is the earliest site of late *Homo sapiens* so far known in China and also in all East Asia.

浙江余姚田螺山
河姆渡文化遗址

*TIANLUOSHAN SITE OF THE HEMUDU CULTURE
IN YUYAO, ZHEJIANG*

田螺山遗址位于余姚市三七镇相岙村,在一个名为田螺山的小山头周围。遗址总面积约30000平方米,西南距河姆渡遗址7公里。在该遗址地下2至3米深处,保存着一个完整的河姆渡文化古村落,形成的时间跨度在1500年以上。2004年2~7月,由浙江省文物考古研究所主持,并联合宁波市文物考古研究所、河姆渡遗址博物馆专业人员,开展首期发掘工作,发掘面积为300平方米。

发掘区处在整个遗址范围的西北部,即田螺山西南侧。地层堆积最厚350厘米左右。目前主要分为8个地层,其中,第3~8层大致相当于河姆渡遗址第2~4层。除最西边的T103已发掘到生土层以外,其他探方均暂停在第7层表面。从地层堆积、遗迹和遗物可以看出,田螺山遗址的形成至少可以分为三个较长的阶段,约相当于河姆渡遗址的第2~4层。

田螺山遗址的第3、4层内基本未见有机质遗物,陶器以灰褐色泥质陶、红褐色夹砂陶为主。器形中陶釜与陶鼎共存,还有少量石器和玉器。在第4层下,出现了比较密集的小土坑和带垫板(木础)的柱坑。前者的坑内有薄薄的淤沙层和一些橡子残留,它们可能是食物储藏坑。后者的坑口形状多呈方形、圆形,其底部常有多层垫板。如在其中一个柱坑内,错向摞叠着6层木板,总厚度达50厘米。一系列的柱坑遗迹表明,至少在河姆渡文化第二期,即距今6000多年以前,河姆渡先民已掌握了干栏式木构建筑的营造技术。

第5层下的遗迹较少,但在T203的偏西位置,出土了数座墓葬。它们位于居住区附近,均没有明显的墓坑、葬具和随葬品,多数肢骨残缺不全,墓

田螺山遗址的地理环境
Geographic environments
of the Tianluoshan site

T103 ⑥层下的木构遗迹,为伴出木桨的木构河埠头(码头)
Remains of a timber structure below Layer T103⑥,
i.e. the ruined timber wharf yielding a wooden oar

出土于 T103 ⑦层堆积近底部的一支木桨
Wooden oar from the bottom of Layer T103 ⑦

主多为少年和青壮年。这些墓可能是二次葬。

在第 6 层以下堆积中,出现了大量的树枝树叶、菱角、橡子、芡实、葫芦、酸枣、炭化米粒、

动物碎骨等,反映出遗址早期更加温暖湿润的生存环境。在第 6 层下出土了排列整齐、加工规整的众多方体木柱,其边长多为 20 多厘米,少数的边长在 40 厘米以上。它们打破第 7、8 层,是早期木构建筑遗迹,属于两个以上的建筑单元。这组建筑遗迹的年代为河姆渡文化二期偏早、一期偏晚阶段。

最西边的探方 T103 内,在第 6 层下也发现了早期木构遗迹,由两根横卧的粗大木材和一系列小木桩构成。在其附近出土了 2 件完好的木桨和一块残桨叶。该遗迹可能是一处临近河湖的小码头或独木桥。

本次发掘出土各类文物近 1000 件,质地有陶、石、玉、骨、角、牙、木等。其中有些器物是以前少见或没有出土过的,如刻画着人脸的陶釜支脚、象

在 T103 ⑦层内出土的一件刻纹陶器
Incised pattern pottery vessel from Layer T103 ⑦

饰人面纹的陶釜支脚
Human face design pottery stand for *fu* cauldron

象首形陶塑残件
Fragment of a pottery sculpture in the shape of an elephant-head

头形陶塑残块、刻画动物图案的夹炭黑陶器、夹炭红衣陶盘口釜、形体高大(高约90厘米)的双耳深腹夹炭陶罐等。在一个灰坑内还出土了一堆萤石、燧石制品,由39件块状原料或半成品、2件燧石质钻具组成。另外还有约9万块陶片和保存上好的各种动植物遗存。

　　田螺山遗址是迄今为止发现的河姆渡文化中地面环境条件最好、地下遗址比较完整的一处依山傍水式的古村落遗址。该遗址的发掘,是继河姆渡、鲻山遗址之后,河姆渡文化早期遗址的又一重要发现。本次发掘初步探明了河姆渡文化早期聚落遗址在姚江流域的分布情况,为该遗址的有效保护赢得了宝贵时间和科学依据。

　　另外,在距地表5米以下的地下山坡表面,发现了一些微粒木炭。这为寻找7000年以前的古人类遗存、揭开河姆渡文化的起源之谜提供了重要线索。

部分小件骨角器和玉石器
Small-sized bone, antler, jade and stone artifacts

在 H9 内发现的 41 件萤石和燧石制品
41 fluorite and flint artifacts discovered in Ash-pit H9

The Tianluoshan site lies round Mt. Tianluo at Sanqi Town of Yuyao City, 7 km northeast of the Hemudu site, and occupies an area of about 30,000 sq m. At a depth of 2 − 3 m below the ground, there remain the intact ruins of an ancient village, the formation of which covered more than 1,500 years. In February to July 2004, the Zhejiang Provincial Institute of Cultural Relics and Archaeology carried out the first season of excavation on the site, revealing an area of 300 sq m.

The stratigraphic deposits and cultural contents of the Tianluoshan site show a relatively steady developmental course of the Hemudu culture without clear missing links. The excavators revealed below the sixth layers two groups of settlement vestiges different in nature, i.e. remains of neat timber houses and those of a wharf on the western side of the houses. They suggest that at the latest by Phase II of Hemudu culture, i.e. the sixth millennium BP, the Hemudu people had mastered the building techniques of pile-dwellings, such as pit digging, board laying, and pole erecting. At the stage under discussion, this type of building became larger in size and mature in technology.

Moreover, a distinct drop in elevation was detected between the earlier deposits and the later ones within the eastern and western parts of the excavated area, with the earlier covered by a thick layer of silt. This distinctive stratigraphic evidence indicates forcefully that the sea level in the Hemudu area rose rapidly round 6000 BP and natural and cultural conditions changed abruptly. Thus it offers an opening for explaining the distinct difference between the early and late remains of the Hemudu culture.

The various cultural relics discovered in this season of excavation total about 760 pieces. A number of them have rare counterparts among the previous finds, and considerably enrich our understanding of the Hemudu culture's contents. They include pottery stands with incised human faces, used for supporting *fu* cauldrons, red-slipped dish-mouthed pottery *fu* of charcoal containing ware, double-eared deep-bellied high pottery jars of this ware, intact wooden oars, and piled up fluorite and flint artifacts.

河北易县
北福地史前遗址

PREHISTORIC BEIFUDI SITE IN YIXIAN COUNTY, HEBEI

北福地遗址位于河北省易县西南 12.5 公里处的北福地村,处在太行山脉东麓与河北平原的接壤地带,地貌属于低山丘陵间的宽阔河谷,中易水由西向东横穿谷底。2003~2004 年,河北省文物研究所对北福地遗址进行了连续两年的考古发掘。已探明的遗址面积约 3 万平方米,文化内涵主要是新石器时代的文化遗存,又可分为三个时期。

北福地一期遗存是此次发掘的重要发现。遗迹有灰坑、房址和祭祀场。房址保存较完整的有 10 座,均为半地穴式,平面形状分为方形和近圆形两种。室内地面中央残存红烧土灶面,周围分布有柱洞。以 F1 为例,平面近圆角方形,南北长 3.9、东西宽 3.85、深 0.45~0.5 米。门道设在北部,呈长条形斜坡状,宽 0.9、残长 0.4 米。居住面为红褐色硬土,比较平整。房址填土中出土遗物非常丰富,包括天然砾石块、石料、各种类型的石制品、陶器残片、刻陶面具和面饰作品残片、胡桃等。

祭祀场平面近长方形,东西长 10.8、南北宽 8.4 米,总面积 90 余平方米。从保存较好的西北部观察,其构造应是直接挖建于生土之上,现存深 20 余厘米,地面较平整。场内祭祀遗迹主要是直腹陶罐、磨制石器、玉器、小石雕、水晶等 90 多件物

北福地史前遗址远景.
A distant view of the prehistoric Beifudi site.

F4
House-foundation F4

考古人员工作情形
Archaeologists at work

品的分组堆积,其中以中小型直腹罐和各种磨制石器为主。有的小型直腹罐体积较小,实际上是陶杯。石器中有一件通体磨光的大型石耜,长达46厘米,可能是迄今为止所发现的形体最大者,制作非常精致。玉器数量较少,仅发现玦、匕两种器形。祭祀物品的堆放以平地铺排为主,似乎分为若干个组合。祭祀物品之间的填土和祭祀场覆土均为深褐色土,杂含灰白色土,剖面观察有层理,质硬,较纯净,极少含有陶器残片等其他遗物。

出土遗物主要是石器和陶器。石器以磨制石器为主,有相当数量的细石器。陶器的陶质均为夹云母陶,未见泥质陶。陶色以灰褐色为主,色多不纯,

有灰色或黑色斑块。纹饰主要是刻划或压印的几何纹,种类有折线、斜线等,多饰于直腹罐口沿下一周。器形主要有直腹罐与支脚两种。直腹罐又分为大中小型,形制基本一致,均为方唇,直口,直壁或斜直壁,平底,口径一般大于通高,口沿下均有纹饰。支脚为倒靴形,陶质与纹饰同于直腹罐。

刻陶假面面具和面饰作品残片发现较多,完整或基本完整者10余件。多见于房址,其次是灰坑。在F1出土的陶片中,面具或面饰陶片约占总数的10%。面具原料均为直腹罐片,以腹部片为主,其次是底片,边缘有切割修整的痕迹。假面面具的大小与真人面部相同,面饰作品则一般在10厘米左

右。平面浅浮雕，单面雕刻，具体技法为阳刻、阴刻、镂空相结合。多用减地法刻出凹面与凸面，再用阴刻法勾勒出线条。图案内容有人面、兽面(包括猪、猴、猫科动物)等。艺术风格兼具写实性、象征性和装饰性。据我们推测，刻陶假面面具可能是祭祀或巫术驱疫时的辅助神器，用来装扮神祇或祖先。这批刻陶面具和面饰是目前所见年代最早、保存最完整的史前面具。一期遗存的绝对年代为距今8000至7000年间，其年代与兴隆洼文化、磁山文化相当，在地域上填补了这两支文化之间的空白，为研究三者之间的关系提供了新依据。

北福地二期遗存的遗迹有灰坑和房址。保存较完整的房址发现2座，形制均为方形半地穴式，室内靠近墙壁分布有柱洞。遗物主要是石器和陶器。石器以各种类型的磨制石器为主，细石器少见。陶器的陶质以夹砂夹云母红褐色陶为主，其次是泥质红陶和灰陶。器表以素面为主，纹饰有少量的刻划纹、刷抹线纹等。器形主要是釜、支脚、红顶钵、小口双耳壶等。北福地二期遗存的文化面貌与镇江营一期晚段、南杨庄一期等近似，相对年代亦应大体相当，略早于后冈一期文化，为后冈一期文化的直接来源。

北福地三期遗存未见完整的文化层堆积，仅发现少量灰坑。陶器以双耳罐、敛口钵最为典型，其文化面貌与雪山一期和镇江营三期遗存相似，年代亦应大体相当。

一期陶罐
Pottery jar of Phase I

二期陶釜
Pottery *fu* cauldron of Phase II

一期陶刻面具
Incised pottery mask of Phase I

一期陶刻面具
Incised pottery mask of Phase I

一期祭祀场出土的石器
Stone implements from the sacrificial
place of Phase I

The Beifudi site is situated on a terrace on the northern bank of the middle Yishui River in Yixian County, Hebei, lying on the hilly land at the eastern foot of the Taihang Mountains. In 2003 − 2004, the Hebei Provincial Institute of Cultural Relics carried out here archaeological excavation in an area of above 1,200 sq m. As is known from the excavation, the site occupies 30,000 sq m in total area and has 0.5 − 1 m thick, complex cultural layers, which contain mainly Neolithic remains, and also relics of the Shang, Zhou, Warring States, Han, Liao and Jin periods.

Judging from stratigraphic deposits and unearthed data, the Neolithic remains can be divided into three phases, which are represented by pottery jars and stands, cauldrons, bowls and stands, and double-bellied jars and double-eared pots respectively. According to ^{14}C dating, the first phase goes back to c. 7000 − 8000 BP, belonging to the early Neolithic.

The main vestiges of Phase I are ash-pits and house-foundations. The latter are rather dense in distribution and orderly in layout, and must be remains of a prehistoric village. The more complete foundations belong to ten semi-subterranean houses with a rectangular, sub-quadrate or sub-round plan. The pottery vessels unearthed all contain mica, and no pure clay ware has been found. The surface is basically brown, varying from gray-, deep- to red- and black-brown, and deep gray can be seen in some cases. These colors are usually impure, and gray and black spots occur frequently. The decorations include incised or stamped meanders, diagonals and other geometric patterns, which are largely made in a circle below the rim. The main types are the jar and stand.

Among the pottery objects are numbers of fragments with incised human faces or animal masks, including over ten intact or restorable. Moreover, a sacrificial place was found to be 10.8 m long from the west to the east and 8.4 m wide from the north to the south. It yielded more than 90 artifacts, such as medium- and small-sized pottery *yu* vessels, various polished stone implements, turquoise ornaments, jade objects, stone statuettes and crystals. It can be inferred that people might have attended the sacrificial activities held there with masks on the face.

The remains of Phase II consist also of ash-pits and semi-subterranean house-foundations. The unearthed objects fall into pottery vessels and stone tools. The former finds are mainly of sandy and mica-containing reddish-brown ware, and also of red or gray clay ware. Their surface is often plain, and incised and rubbed patterns occur in some cases. In form there are principally cauldrons and stands, red-rimmed bowls, and small-mouthed double-eared pots.

Going back to an early period, the vestiges and objects of Phase I constitute a group of early remains that dates later only than the Nanzhuangtou site among the Neolithic discoveries recorded so far in North China. They provided new data for studying the origins of the early Neolithic culture and dry farming in this region.

河南灵宝西坡遗址
发现仰韶文化中期特大房址

A SURPRISINGLY LARGE HOUSE-FOUNDATION OF THE MIDDLE YANGSHAO CULTURE DISCOVERD ON THE XIPO SITE IN LINGBAO, HENAN

西坡遗址位于河南省灵宝市阳平镇，坐落在黄土塬上，南依小秦岭，北面黄河，总面积约40万平方米。2000～2002年初，中国社会科学院考古研究所与河南省文物考古研究所等单位组成联合考古队，对该遗址进行了三次发掘，在遗址的中心部位发现一座仰韶文化中期大型半地穴房址（F105），其室内面积达204平方米。2004年4～7月，联合考古队对遗址进行了第四次发掘，发掘面积约800平方米，揭露出仰韶文化中期又一座大型的半地穴房址——F106。

F106开口在仰韶文化中期文化层下，局部被晚期墓葬M5、M6等打破。房址内堆积分为4层。其中最下层是房屋倒塌堆积，包含墙体抹泥残块和

夯土墙体残块。居住面上未见任何遗物。房址结构颇为复杂，包括半地穴、木结构遗迹和地面上墙体三部分。

半地穴部分大致呈四边形，南壁长15.7、东壁长14、西壁长14.3米。北壁外弧，被门道分割成东西两段，分别长约8.5和8.8米，与东西两壁呈108°钝角。居住面面积约240平方米。墙体保存高度0.4～0.8米，上面是平整的抹泥台面，宽约0.6米。半地穴墙壁由夯土筑成，其中居住面以下部分填黄色夯土；居住面及其以上部分，外侧是棕色夯土，内侧为青灰色草拌泥，表面涂朱。

居住面加工考究，厚约25.5厘米，有7层。自下而上分别是青灰色草拌泥、黄色硬土、棕色草拌

西坡遗址发掘现场
Xipo site in excavation

13

F106 鸟瞰图
A bird-eye's view of House—foundation F106

14

F106半地穴墙壁，墙面涂朱
Red-painted wall of the F106 semi-subterranean

F106室内火塘
Fireplace in F106

泥、青灰色夹料礓石抹泥、青灰色草拌泥、棕色草拌泥和含大量料礓石的坚硬地面。地面涂朱。北墙中部开有斜坡式门道，朝向东北，方向24°，长6.8米。门道两壁有厚约15厘米的抹泥。火塘正对门道，开口近圆形，直径1.45米。直壁，平底，深约0.9米。火塘面对门道处，凸出一弧形矮坎，坎下塘壁上开有一弧顶暗道，由居住面下通向门道方向。因被M5打破，难以了解其完整结构。

壁柱柱洞现存41个，柱间距0.4～4.6米，柱洞直径多为25～30厘米。室内柱有4个，匀称地分布在室内对角线上，距离其对应的屋角均约4米。柱坑近圆形，直径约1米。位于东北角的柱坑(N1)底部有平整的础石，直径约26厘米，可作为柱径的参考。

外墙与半地穴墙壁平行，南壁长17、东壁长14.7、西壁长14.5米，北壁东、西段分别长9和9.4米。保存高度0.1～0.3米，平均厚度0.6米，内侧抹有5厘米厚的草拌泥。外墙内面积约270平方米，含墙体约296平方米。外墙也是夯筑而成。在外墙与半地穴墙上台面交界处的下部，发现立柱的痕迹，估计柱槽内曾立柱，作为夯土时的依托。

F106的建造程序大致如下：先挖出半地穴墙槽，在墙槽内竖立壁柱，并用黄色土夯实。再以棕色土夯筑半地穴墙体，直至与半地穴墙槽齐平。在墙体内侧挖出半地穴，门道和火塘也同时挖成。竖立室内柱，完成整个木结构。在墙体外侧约20厘米处，挖槽埋立细柱，然后依托细柱夯筑外墙。拔走细柱，将留下的沟槽填实，并修整出墙体上的台面。用青灰色草拌泥铺抹居住面第一层、半地穴墙壁及其上部台面、外墙内侧。铺设居住面其他层，全部完成后，将居住面和半地穴墙壁内侧涂朱。最后葺顶，架设门道顶棚。

F105和F106使我们认识到，早在仰韶文化中期，大型的半地穴房屋建设已包括多项程序，要耗费大量的人力物力。F106与F105同处遗址的中心，间隔约50米，两座房屋不仅有居住功能，还应是聚落内的重要公共活动场所。这是仰韶文化中期社会复杂化的一个标志，对理解早期国家在这一地区的形成有重要启示。

In April to July 2004, the archaeological team jointly organized by the Institute of Archaeology, CASS, and the Henan Provincial Institute of Cultural Relics and Archaeology carried out the fourth excavation on the Lingbao Xipo site, in the center of the ruins. In the excavated area of about 800 sq m., they revealed a surprisingly large house-foundation and two ash-pits of the middle Yangshao culture and three ash-pits of the late Yangshao, and brought to light a number of cultural relics.

The house-foundation (F106) is quite good in condition and represents a sub-rectangular semi-subterranean building. It is rather complex in structure, consisting of a semi-subterranean, a wooden frame and remaining walls on the ground. The former measures about 15.7, 14, 14.3 and 17.3 m for the southern, eastern, western and northern sides respectively and has a floor area of about 240 sq m. The northern wall arcs outward. Its middle is furnished with a ramping doorway, which points to the northeast with an azimuth of 24°, and extends and gradually narrows from the inside to the exit, measuring about 6.8 m in length and 0.45 − 0.8 m in width. The aboveground walls are 0.4 − 0.8 m in remaining height and about 0.6 m in width. Their top is plastered with clay, and the surface along with the floor is painted in red.

The floor is made elaborately and measures 25.5 cm in total thickness. It consists of seven layers, which are, from the lower to the upper, straw-mixed livid clay, hard yellow earth, straw-mixed brown clay, lime-concretion-mixed livid clay, straw-mixed livid clay, straw-mixed brown clay, and red-painted hard surface with lime concretion in a great quantity respectively. The fireplace is directed to the doorway. It is about 2 m apart from the door, has a sub-round plan, straight walls and a level bottom, and measures about 1.45 m in diameter and 0.9 m in depth. The walls and bottom are hard and brown. The side closer to the door has an arc-shaped low platform, below which a vaulted underground way extends towards the doorway.

The wooden structure is represented by the remaining holes of wall and indoor posts. The former remains number 41 and measure largely 25-30 cm in diameter. The latter number four and are neatly distributed on the indoor diagonals. Judging by the earth fillings and

在西坡遗址 H6 内发现的研磨朱砂用的磨棒
Roller for cinnabar grinding from Ash−pit H6 of the Xipo site

西坡遗址出土的白衣黑彩陶碗
Pottery bowl with white slip and black design from the Xipo site

other traces in the post-holes, all the posts were moved away by the dwellers, and the sub-round post-holes about 1 m in diameter seen in excavation must have been formed when the posts were moved.

The aboveground walls are parallel to and a little longer than the sides of the subterranean, measuring about 10 − 30 cm in remaining height and 40 − 95 cm in thickness. The inner side is plastered with 5 cm thick straw-mixed clay. The area within these walls is about 270 sq m, or 296 sq m if the wall body is included.

Another semi-subterranean (F105) in the center of the site is also surprisingly large-sized and stands about 50 m apart from the former. The mutual correspondence of the two houses is of great value to understanding the layout of the whole site.

山西芮城
清凉寺庙底沟二期墓地

QINGLIANGSI CEMETERY OF THE MIAODIGOU II CULTURE IN RUICHENG, SHANXI

芮城县位于山西西南黄河拐弯处,清凉寺墓地位于芮城县的东北部,发现于1955年,1965年被公布为山西省重点文物保护单位。2003年深秋到2004年初冬,山西省考古研究所与运城市文物局、芮城县文物局联合,对清凉寺墓地进行了田野考古发掘。

清凉寺墓地在一条南北向的狭窄台塬上,中部是元大德七年(1303年)始建的清凉寺。墓葬区位于清凉寺东北,是一块较低平的区域,海拔高度620余米。其东部为坡头遗址,墓葬区与遗址区之间有一条冲沟,泉水终年流淌。

本次发掘共清理墓葬262座。墓葬开口在表土层或垫土层下,均为长方形土坑竖穴,有大型墓、小型墓之分。大型墓长2.3~2.6、宽1.3~1.8米,墓内死者一般为成人,头向正西。多数为仰身直肢一次葬,墓主人身上涂朱和墓内撒放朱砂的现象比较普遍。

从墓地的中部向东的范围内,大型墓葬排列十分整齐,南北成行、东西成列,形制也比较接近。但近墓地西部,有相当一部分墓葬存在打破关系。

清凉寺墓地的位置(自东南向西北摄)
Location of the Qingliangsi cemetery (photo from southeast to northwest)

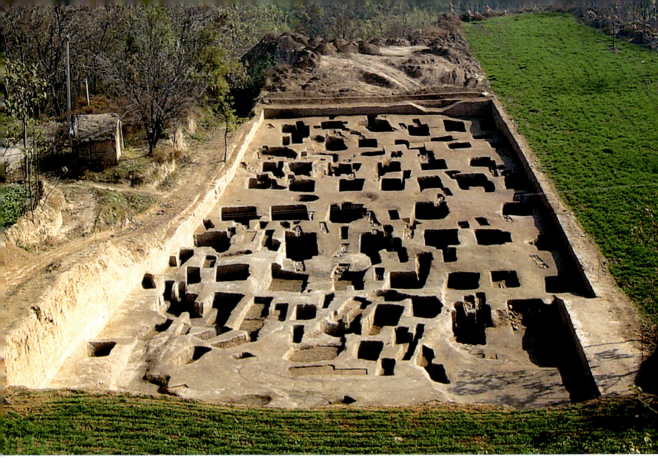

清凉寺墓地的发掘情况(自西向东摄)
Qingliangsi cemetery in excavation
(photo from west to east)

M46
Tomb M46

　　大型墓大多有熟土二层台,一半以上的墓葬还有小孩殉葬。墓葬反映的情况十分复杂,墓内骨骼被扰乱的达90%,因此,骨骼不全或位置错乱的现象比比皆是。如有的墓主下半身尚保持在原位,但上半身则翻转过来,肋骨更被弃置于一侧。有的墓内是十分散乱的人骨,还有些墓内的头骨或肢骨与墓主人并非一个个体。这些墓葬除极个别者外,均没有现代盗挖的迹象,形成这种现象的原因是什么,目前尚未达成共识。

　　小型墓发现较多,一般长约2、宽0.5~0.8米,墓内死者多为仰身直肢,头向正西,未见殉人,也没有二层台。

　　在所有发掘的墓葬中,有随葬品的墓葬约占三分之一,每座墓中随葬品的数量从1件到16件不等。器物的摆放位置不太统一,多在墓主人头部、两臂、腹部或下肢一侧。

　　随葬品以玉石器为主,但种类较少,主要是玉璧、环、钺、石刀,其他还有石斧、小玉饰等。除玉石器外,还有少量的陶器和骨簪。鳄鱼骨板、兽

M51 与 M61
Tombs M51 and M61

M79
Tomb M79

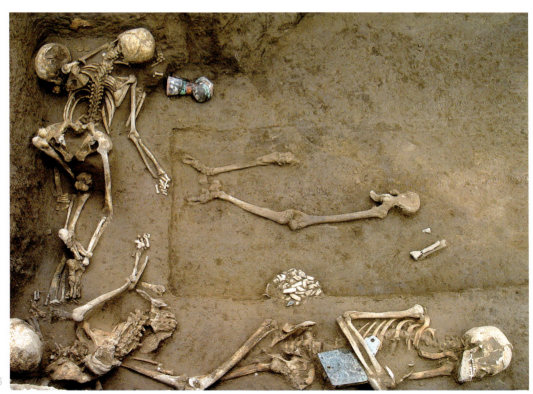

M146
Tomb M146

牙和猪下颌骨等与财富、地位相关的遗物，一般发现于大型墓中。M52虽然已经被盗扰，但墓内出土一件玉琮和部分兽牙，墓主人可能是首领级人物。此外，M100出土的牙璧也较特殊。

　　清凉寺墓地的墓葬可被划分为三个阶段。其中大型墓排列整齐有序，应该是属于同一个阶段、同一部族的墓地。被它们打破的墓葬一般是小型墓，其年代早于大型墓。此外还有少数打破大型墓的小墓，它们属于墓地最晚的阶段。这批墓葬均属于庙底沟二期文化的最后阶段。

玉琮
Jade *cong* cubic object round inside and square outside

The Qingliangsi cemetery is located in the northeast of Ruicheng County, Shanxi Province. It was discovered in 1955 and was excavated by the Shanxi Provincial Institute of Archaeology in the early winter of 2003 through 2004. Northeast of Qingliangsi, the archaeologists excavated 262 tombs.

These graves are all rectangular earthen pits with the opening beneath the surface soil or bedded soil layer. The dead are largely adults lying in an extended supine position, head pointing to the due west.

The tombs can be divided into larger- and smaller-sized. The former often contain second-tier platforms and human victims-children. The human skeletons are incomplete or disturbed, which reflects a complex condition. The smaller tombs are enough for one corpse only and have a few funeral objects in some cases.

The grave goods range one to 16 pieces for one burial, and greatly vary in quality and shape. They are put at the head, both arms, underbelly, etc. Of them the jade and stone objects form the greatest proportion, though their types are not so many. The main types are the *cong* cubic object round inside ad square outside, *bi* disc, ring, *yue* battle-axe and knife; the rest include square objects and small ornaments. A few tombs yielded crocodiles' bones, bone artifacts, pigs' mandibles and pottery vessels.

Judging from the intrusion of tombs and the features of part of the pottery, the cemetery was used in three stages, all belonging to the final phase of Miaodigou II

玉牙璧
Lobed jade *bi*

culture. The excavation brought about important results. It provided valuable data for studying the evolution of ancient culture in the juncture of Shaanxi, Shanxi and Henan and the origin of ancient Chinese civilization. Meanwhile, it put forward some new research subjects. The material of the present excavation has not been systematized, and its understanding calls for further deepening.

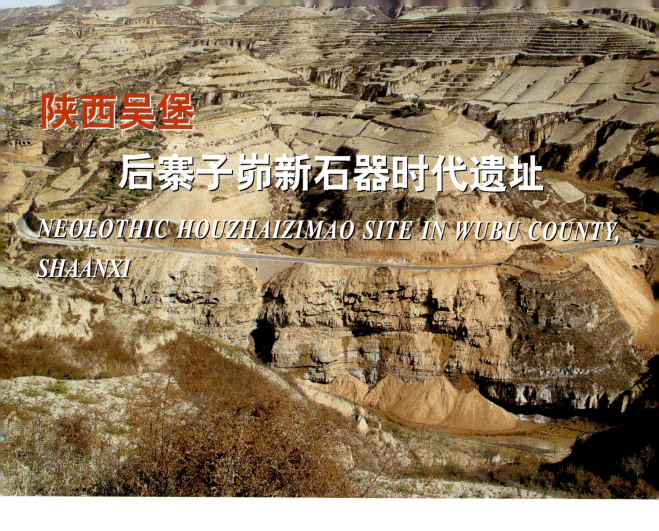

陕西吴堡
后寨子峁新石器时代遗址

NEOLOTHIC HOUZHAIZIMAO SITE IN WUBU COUNTY, SHAANXI

后寨子峁位于陕西省吴堡县辛家沟乡李家河村西北,由三座山梁连接而成,遗址就分布于这三座山梁上。遗址西侧有一条名为清河沟的小河,由西北向东南流淌。2004年8~12月,陕西省考古研究所对该遗址进行了勘探、发掘。遗址面积约21万平方米,本次发掘面积近3000平方米。共发现房址70余处(已发掘48座)、灰坑近20座(已发掘13座),并发掘陶窑1座、石围墙及墙外壕沟各两段,主要是庙底沟二期至龙山文化早期的遗存。

在一号山梁与三号山梁相连的马鞍部,有一道西北—东南走向的石围墙。墙体外侧地势较低,略似壕沟。围墙和壕沟使地势较低的一号山梁形成一个相对独立的整体。围墙残长35、残高0.5~1.8米,均以当地砂页岩石片、石条和石块砌筑而成。墙体表面整齐美观,上部内收呈护坡状,墙体与土坡之间填以土石。石围墙中部偏西北处有5级台阶,应是一号山梁与外部的一条通道。石台阶以内有一座葬有完整狗骨架的圆形坑,当与修建城墙或石台阶的某种宗教仪式有关。

二号山梁与一号山梁地势相似,临沟的三面山坡上残存有断断续续的石围墙,石围墙外未见人工壕沟。而与三号山梁相连的鞍部也有石围墙,残长约30、残高1-4米。墙外挖有规整的壕沟,深约2~3、口部宽3~3.5米,使得二号山梁也成为一座相对独立的部分,并在壕沟东端留有土台阶与外部相通。三号山梁上未发现石围墙,这可能与其地势最高有关。

本次发掘的48座房址分别位于三座山梁上,其中一号山梁11座、二号山梁22座、三号山梁15座。房址沿山坡层层而建,由下而上形成多排,规模相当宏伟。二号山梁上的房址一直延续至山顶台地上,且房址分布密度较大。房址的建造方式可分为窑洞式、半地穴式、半地穴式与窑洞式相结合的复合式三种,房址的平面形制大致可分为"凸"字形、"甲"字形、"吕"字形、刀把形和不规则形等。

"凸"字形房址一般为窑洞式建筑,由主室和

二号山梁

石墙及壕沟

二号山梁

石墙及壕沟

一号山梁

后寨子峁遗址地形俯瞰
A vertical view of the geomorphology of the Houzhaizimao site

沿山坡而建的房址
House-founda-
tions along the
hill-slops

带有精美地画的"吕"字形房址
"吕"-shaped house-foun-
dation with find ground
painting

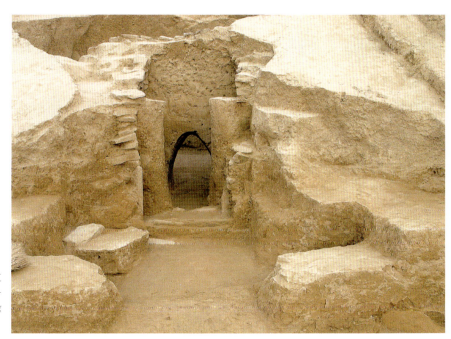

带门洞、立柱的"吕"字形房址
"吕"-shaped house-foun-
dation with door-opening
and posts

门道组成。主室平面多为近圆形或圆角方形,顶部虽已坍塌,但从室壁残存的弧度分析,应当是穹隆顶。门道为内宽外窄的过道,多为拱形顶。室内地面和墙裙多为平整光滑的白灰面,主室正中或门道一侧一般有灶坑。室内面积多为10平方米左右,主室复原高度约3~4米。此类房址约占所发掘房址总数的四分之一,规模一般较小。

"甲"字形房址只发现一座,位于三号山梁东南部。与"凸"字形房址的形制接近,房址门外有一条很长的坑道,宽约1.2、长约15米。

"吕"字形房址均为复合式建筑,由前室、过道和后室组成。后室一般是主室,为窑洞式建筑,直接掏于生土断崖之中。穹隆顶,平面有圆形、圆角方形和后圆前方等形制,面积较大,一般在15~

23

房址后室白灰墙裙底部的红色条带
Red stripe at the base of the lime dado of the rear room

20平方米之间。后室的地面和墙裙多为平整的白灰面,地面正中有一处黑彩绘制的地画,为灶坑或火盘。多呈圆形或圆角方形,边长(或直径)约0.5～1.4米,中间有烧火痕迹和灰烬。墙裙底部与地面相交的地方有一周深红色的彩绘条带。过道窄长,地面、墙裙也饰以白灰面和红色彩绘,在墙裙顶部的白灰面上,有一周用手蘸黑彩抹划的痕迹。前室一般为半地穴式建筑,平面为方形或长方形。地面和墙壁以平整的砂页岩石片砌筑,面积多在3～6平方米之间。前室、过道和后室之间有窄门或立柱相隔,使三部分相互连通而又相对独立。房址总面

积多在20～30平方米之间,其房址数目在所发掘的房址中约占四分之一。

刀把形房址只在二号山梁上发现一座,由近方形主室和窄长的通道组成。主室为窑洞式建筑,边长约2.5～3米,面积约8平方米。室内地面以大型石片铺砌,地面正中石板上凿有一个直径22厘米的圆形的洞,口大底尖,可能是储存火种罐或尖底器的坑洞。

48座房址之间存在着明显的组群关系。如三号山梁的F3与F6,二者朝向同一个方向,门前原有土坯铺设的道路相连。F6门外的斜坡和土踏步

边长1.5米的大型地画,为灶坑或火盘
Large-sized ground painting 1.5 m long for each side, remaining of a fireplace

刀把形房址
L-shaped house-foundation

拐向F3，而且两座房址门外有一处共用的院落
(坪)，院落地面为大面积的踩踏面。这表明F3、F6
之间有着极为密切的关系，房屋主人亦应存在着亲
密的血缘或社会关系。三号山梁的2座房址内发现
有被肢解的人骨，经鉴定均为青壮年男性，可能是
被处死的战俘或是该部族内部违规之人。

　　后寨子峁遗址是陕北地区第一处大规模揭露的
史前大型聚落遗址，它布局独特，房屋形制丰富，
组群关系清晰，为研究陕北地区新石器时代聚落形
态演变以及环境变迁提供了实物资料。

The Houzhaizimao site lies in Wubu County,
Yulin City, Shaanxi Province, on the eastern
bank of the Qinghegou Stream that runs from northwest
to southeast. It spreads on three hills joining together in
the shape of the character " 人," extending from the
foot to the summit and occupying an area of 210,000 sq
m in total. In August to December 2004, the Shaanxi
Institute of Archaeology carried out on the site the first
season of extensive excavation, which covered nearly
3,000 sq m. The main remains belong to the Miaodigou
II to the early Longshan culture.

The site consists of three parts that occupy the three
hills respectively. The two parts on the lower Nos. 1
and 2 hills were discovered to have had a stone enclosure
each. The remains so far found on the three hills
include 70 house-foundations (48 excavated), nearly
20 ash-pits (13 excavated), one pottery-firing kiln-
site, two sections of stone enclosures and two sections
of moats. The unearthed objects fall into pottery vessels,
stone implements and bone artifacts. The pottery is
similar to that from the Suide Xiaoguandao, Shenmu
Zhengzemao I and Inner Mongolia Ashan III and
Guandi III sites, and might be included into the Ashan
culture. But the Houzhaizimao site shows certain
features of its own in cultural aspect and settlement
pattern, and constitutes an important large-sized site in
prehistoric North China. It maybe represents a new
culture or type in this region.

山东荏平
教场铺龙山文化城址

JIAOCHANGPU CITY-SITE OF THE LONGSHAN CULTURE IN CHIPING, SHANDONG

教场铺龙山文化城址位于山东省聊城市荏平县乐平铺镇，北距荏平县城22.5公里。该遗址发现于1996年。自2000年开始，中国社会科学院考古研究所山东队、山东省文物考古研究所、聊城市文物局联合对该遗址进行发掘。经过四次发掘，共清理灰坑600余座、房址50余座、窑址7座，出土各类遗物近万件。2004年4～7月，在对教场铺遗址进行的第四次发掘中，我们发现了属于山东龙山文化晚期的城墙遗存，和一批与城墙相关的奠基坑、祭祀坑。

城址平面为东西略长、南北稍窄的椭圆形，东西长约230、南北宽约180米，城内面积近5万平方米。为了解城墙的结构、建筑方法和年代，我们发掘了三条探沟，编号分别为TG2、TG3和TG4。

TG2位于北城墙的中段偏东。城墙分为早晚两期。一期城墙为地面起建，现存高度0.75～1.6米，顶宽17、底宽17.5米。城墙内外两侧均有壕沟，应该是两侧取土，向中间堆筑而成。其外侧壕沟作为护城壕使用。内侧壕沟贴近城墙一侧较为陡直，另一侧呈缓坡状，与城内地面相衔接。一期城墙采用黄沙，混合红色黏土分层夯筑，夯层厚5～8厘米，夯窝不明显。该城墙用

TG2城墙剖面
Section of a city wall in Excavation Square TG2

10号祭祀坑
Sacrificial Pit 10

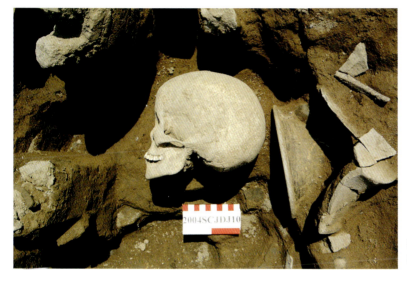

祭祀坑内的人头骨
Human skull in a sacrificial pit

土没有经过人为扰动，夯土内几乎不见陶片，较为纯净。由此推测，这是当时人始到此地居住时所筑之城墙。二期城墙斜压在一期城墙的内外两侧和顶部，现存高度0.7～3.2米，顶宽27、底宽近30米。二期城墙的建筑方法略有不同，城墙直接夯筑在一期城墙两侧的壕沟上，且夯筑前并未对沟内的淤土进行清理。淤土经间接夯打后，同样十分坚硬。

TG3内的二期城墙较薄。它并未叠压在一期城墙的护城壕上，而是在贴近城墙根部向下开挖一剖面呈U形的沟，作为基槽，然后向上夯打而成。夯层厚20余厘米，局部夯窝明显，夯窝直径3～5厘米，应为棍夯。在夯层之间还发现了被夯碎的完整陶器，这应是城墙奠基的一种形式。

根据以上发现我们推测，该遗址是一处高于当时地表的沙丘，第一批定居者到达遗址后即开始修建城墙（即一期城墙）。一期城墙使用了一段时间后，城内居民再次对城墙进行修筑，形成了二期城墙。由于遗址范围内经历长期的人类活动，因此二期城墙的用土多为灰土，且包含有大量的陶片等人工制成品。

我们在两期城墙之间发现了5座祭祀坑。8号祭祀坑（JSK8）位于北城墙东段，被第二期城墙叠

8号祭祀坑
Sacrificial Pit 8

鸟首足陶盆形鼎
Basin-shaped pottery *ding* tripod with
bird-head-shaped legs

陶鬲
Pottery *li* tripod

压，又打破第一期城墙。平面呈勺形，长径2.8、短径2.25米。斜直壁，平底。坑内填土经过夯打，比较坚硬。坑底部出土大量陶片，包括罐、壶等，均为典型的龙山文化晚期陶器。

在JSK8与JSK10内均大量存在不能完全复原的陶器，有些仅缺底部或腹部。对此我们推测，在筑第二期城墙之前，首先挖好祭祀坑和奠基坑，然后将陶器、肢解的人和动物肢体及其他物品有选择地摆放在这些坑内。而陶器很可能是打碎后分别置于临近的几个坑内，因而在一个遗迹单位内，往往只看到一件器物的某一部分。

城址中还发现了房址、陶窑、灰坑、墓葬等其他遗迹。房址多为平地起建或浅穴式建筑，平面形状有圆形、圆角方形和方形三种。平地起建的房址一般是先夯打房基，然后挖墙基槽，起墙，作顶，抹墙皮，最后铺垫房内地面，墙皮和居住面都要涂抹白灰面。浅穴式建筑一般在墙外还要修建护坡。房址内部结构基本相同，居住面中心设灶，灶的四周立有4根木柱。门道一般位于房的南侧或东南侧，正对着灶。圆形或圆角方形的房屋面积较大，为27～28平方米；方形房屋面积较小，只有16平方米左右。

第四次发掘还获得了一批龙山文化的陶、石、骨、蚌、角器等遗物。陶器中夹砂陶主要有篮纹罐、绳纹罐、方格纹罐、菱形网格纹罐、盆形鼎、罐形鼎、鬶、甗等，泥质陶主要有磨光蛋壳黑陶杯、磨光黑陶三足盘、平底盆、圈足盆、罐、磨光褐陶豆等。其他遗物有蚌刀、蚌镰、蚌铲、骨锥、骨镞、石凿等。值得一提的是，六号祭祀坑内出土了4件卜骨，其中3件有明显的灼痕，这是年代较早的卜骨。

教场铺作为龙山文化晚期的城址，为研究中国古代社会复杂化进程提供了实物资料。

磨光黑陶双耳罐
Double-eared pottery jar of polished black ware

陶圈足盘
Ring-foot pottery dish

The Jiaochangpu city-site of Longshan culture is located at Lepingpu Town of Chiping County in Liaocheng City, Shandong Province, lying 22.5 km to the south of the seat of Chiping County. It was discovered in 1996. Later, the Project Group of "Excavation and Study of the Longshan Culture Jiaochangpu Site in Shandong Chiping" was jointly organized by the Shandong Archacological Team, Institute of Archaeology, CASS, the Shandong Provincial Institute of Cultural Relics and Archaeology, and the Liaocheng Municipal Bureau of Culture. They began excavation on the site from 2000. Through four seasons of excavation, over 600 ash-pits, above 50 houses-foundations and 7 kiln-sites have been revealed, approximately ten thousands of various objects have been brought to light, and the date and nature of the site have been roughly clarified.

In April to July 2004, during the fourth excavation on the Jiaochangpu site, archaeologists discovered remaining walls of late Shandong Longshan culture and a number of foundation laying ceremony and sacrificial pits related to them. Based on the results of drilling and excavation it can be preliminarily believed that the city-site has an oval plan with the major axis pointing to the west and east. It measures about 230 m long from the west to the east and about 180 m wide from the north to the south, occupying an area of approximately 50,000 sq m.

Originally this place must have been a dune higher than the then surrounding ground. As time went on, its first settlers built here the city walls that belong to Phase I as known from the absence of man-made objects in their rammed earth. Later, to make the city-walls higher and thicker, the inhabitants rebuilt them. Thus the Phase II city-walls came into being. As the site went through a long period of man's living, the earth used for building the second phase city-walls were largely ashy and contained quantities of broken artifacts such as shards. Archaeologists discovered between the two phases of city-walls a number of sacrificial remains related to city-wall construction, including five sacrificial pits. Within the city-site, excavators revealed house-foundations, kiln-sites, ash-pits and tombs, as well as plenty of Longshan culture objects.

The discovery of the Jiaochangpu city-site is of great significance. Spatially, the western Shandong region where the site is located was the area where the Dongyi and Huaxia blocs met with each other and the cultural aspect was quite complex. So the reflection of the two blocs' relationship in this region is in the focus of attention. The origin of Chinese civilization was a long course, and the Longshan culture was just the final stage before the formation of civilized society. Some scholars even believe that the Longshan culture already crossed the threshold of incipient civilization. As a group of middle and late Longshan culture ruins, the Jiaochangpu city-site provides material data for researching into the course of ancient Chinese society toward complexity.

浙江平湖
庄桥坟良渚文化墓地

ZHUANGQIAOFEN CEMETERY OF THE LIANGZHU CULTURE IN PINGHU, ZHEJIANG

庄桥坟遗址位于浙江省平湖市林埭镇群丰村，南距平湖市约13公里。这里地处杭嘉湖平原东北部，属北亚热带季风气候，向南5公里即是钱塘江的北海岸线。

2003年6月~2004年10月，浙江省文物考古研究所与平湖市博物馆联合组成考古队，对该遗址进行了发掘，发掘面积为2000平方米。共发现3座良渚文化时期土台，清理灰坑、沟、祭祀坑等遗迹近100处，清理良渚文化中晚期墓葬236座。出土各类随葬品近2600件（组），还有大量的炭化米，以及植物果核和动物骨骸。

经初步调查和钻探，这个聚落遗址的面积可能超过10万平方米。其北部的中心区由较纯的黄斑土堆筑而成，在此发现红烧土墙体，推测这里是居住区。南部则是公共墓地，其布局为由南往北、东西向的若干排墓葬埋葬区。发掘区的东南可能存在农业生产区。

已发现的3个人工土台，呈东西向一字排列。中间土台东西长18.5、南北宽10.75米，面积近200平方米。土台最初用黄斑土堆筑而成，之后不断向

发掘现场局部
Part of the site of excavation

墓葬叠压、打破情形
Superimposition and
intrusion of tombs

M160
Tomb M160

四周扩大，最后使3个土台相连，形成一个面积较
大的平地。在土台扩展的过程中，有意识地安置了
埋狗或猪的祭祀坑。

　墓葬均为土坑竖穴，规模大小不一。最大的是
M138，长3.35、宽0.85米；最小的是M207，长
0.9、宽0.3米。个别墓葬有葬具，大部分墓葬的
葬具不明。除18座墓为东西向、1座墓的头向朝北
外，其余墓葬均呈南北向，头朝南。多为仰身直肢
葬，骨架保存状况较好，其中M77的头骨可以复
原，这为我们做体质人类学研究提供了宝贵资料。

　墓葬集中分布在约1000平方米的墓地范围内，
可分为四大片区。每片都有等级较高的墓葬，而且
随葬品较为丰富，有玉璧或玉钺等玉礼器。在236
座墓葬中，共有56组、160余座墓存在着叠压、打
破关系，最多的一组有10多座墓。12座墓在墓坑

M100 出土的陶器
Pottery from Tomb M100

M19 内的殉狗
Dog victim in Tomb M19

北端殉葬了驯养的成年狗，狗的头骨均朝向墓主人的脚端。从葬具较为清楚的墓葬来看，狗被置于葬具外北端的墓坑内。

在土台上面发现5个狗的祭祀坑，呈东西向或南北向，坑内无其他遗物。在土台西南还发现1个猪的祭祀坑(H18)，呈东西向。从祭祀坑的分布看，它并不从属于某个特定墓葬，而与所在这一片的墓地祭祀活动有关。

良渚时期的灰坑有44个，平面形状多样，大小差异很大。大部分坑内遗物较少，但H31和H70例外。H31出土了一些陶片和较多的有机物，包括木板、木棍、麻绳、苇编，以及葫芦、酸枣、薏米、梨等植物果核和鹿角、猪、鱼等动物骨骸。

在H70内发现一把带木质犁底的组合式分体石犁，通长106厘米，犁尖朝向东南。石犁头由三部分组成，长51、宽44厘米。在木犁底部尾端，有装置犁辕的榫口。这是迄今发现的最早的带木质犁底的石犁，为研究史前农业提供了重要的实物资料。

　　墓内的随葬品多寡不一，少者1件，多者50余件，大部分墓随葬10余件器物。随葬品以陶器为主，还有石、玉、骨角、象牙、木器等。其中陶器1500余件，器形有鼎、豆、双鼻壶、壶、簋、罐、盘、盆、杯、纺轮等，而以双鼻壶最多，这是当地良渚文化的特色。石器主要有钺、镞、有孔石刀、锛、犁、镰、耘田器等。其中石钺的形制比较丰富，

最大的一件石钺高31厘米，穿孔周围有一圈白色胶结物。玉器主要有璧、钺、镯、环、锥形器、坠、珠等，骨角器有镞、锥、靴形器等，象牙器有镯、匕等，木器有篦子。

　　庄桥坟遗址是迄今发现的最大的良渚文化墓地。四大片埋葬区有各自的特点，可能反映了每片区域内死者的血缘关系。每一片区域里都有规模相对较大、等级较高的墓葬。墓葬中随葬品的多寡不一，反映出当时社会已出现贫富分化，但来自同一血缘不同阶层的死者仍可以埋葬在同一区域。

M76部分随葬品出土情形
Funeral objects being unearthed from Tomb M76

M147内出土的玉钺
Jade *yue* battle-axe from Tomb M147

石犁
Stone plough

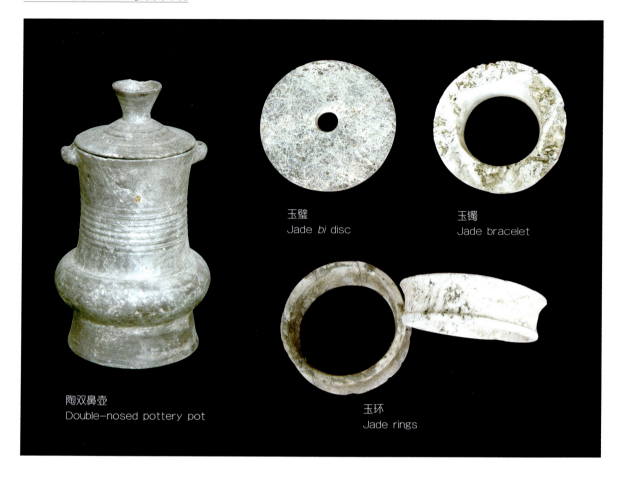

玉璧
Jade *bi* disc

玉镯
Jade bracelet

陶双鼻壶
Double-nosed pottery pot

玉环
Jade rings

The Zhuangqiaofen site lies at Lindai Town in Pinghu County, Zhejiang Province, 5 km north of the northern coastline of the Hangzhou Bay, in the northeast of the Hangjiahu Plain, with the climate belonging to the northern subtropical monsoon zone. It was discovered in May 2003, with the area estimated at above 100,000 sq m. From 1 June 2003 to 13 October 2004, the archaeological team jointly organized by the Zhejiang Provincial Institute of Cultural Relics and Archaeology and the Pinghu Municipal Museum carried out excavation on the site.

In the excavated area of 2,000 sq m, they revealed 3 earthen platforms and nearly 100 ash-pits and -trenches and sacrificial pits of the Liangzhu culture, and 236 tombs of the middle and late Liangzhu.

The tombs are all earthen pits and vary in size, and can be divided into four areas according to their difference in feature. Among them 12 contain dog victims, 18 point to the east and west for the major axis, and some intruded red burnt clay. Superimposition and intrusion cover 56 group of over 160 burials. In the expanding course of the platforms, sacrificial pits were dug to bury dog and pig victims. The human skeletons suggest that the dead belong to various ten-year periods in age and have no great disparity in the proportion of men to women.

The funeral objects fall mainly into pottery, stone, jade, bone, antler, ivory and wooden artifacts, numbering approximately 2,600 pieces/sets. The rest include carbonized rice in a large amount, gourd, wild jujube, Job's tears and pear seeds or stones, deer-antlers and dog-, pig-, and fish-bones. The compound stone plough with a wooden base from Ash-pit H70 is a new find in prehistoric archaeology. It reflects the developmental level of plough farming in the Liangzhu period.

The Zhuangqiaofen cemetery is the largest burial ground recorded so far in the Liangzhu culture. It has considerable significance to understanding the settlement pattern and social structure at that time.

浙江湖州
塔地新石器时代遗址

NEOLITHIC TADI SITE IN HUZHOU, ZHEJIANG

004年3月~2005年1月，为配合农村土地平整项目，浙江省文物考古研究所与湖州市博物馆联合组队，对湖州市千金镇塔地遗址进行抢救性考古发掘，发掘面积近3500平方米。发现并清理马家浜文化、崧泽文化、良渚文化、马桥文化时期的墓葬58座、灰坑130个、房址1座，出土陶、石、玉、骨、木、象牙器等文物800余件。

马家浜文化遗存主要有灰坑与墓葬。灰坑平面多呈不规则形状，多数为堆置生活废弃物的垃圾坑，出土陶腰沿釜、鼎、牛鼻耳罐、甗、豆、侧把盉等遗物。墓葬22座，呈排列有序的4排，集中分布在发掘区的西北部。墓葬均为长方形竖穴土坑，墓坑狭长。填土分为黑褐色和黄褐色两种，从打破关系看，填黄褐色土的墓葬在入埋时间上要早于填黑褐色的。墓内人骨大多保存较好，头向均朝北。葬式有俯身直肢、侧身直肢、仰身直肢和侧身屈肢等多种，面向多数朝西。多数墓葬无随葬品，有6

座墓葬出土了包括玉玦、玉管、骨管串、骨匕、纺轮等在内的随葬品。其中M56被马桥文化灰坑H125打破，仅存头部，葬式不明。头骨面向朝西，除在上、下耳部各发现1件玉玦外，还出有玉管与骨匕各1件。M40墓主为一名25~30岁的女性，头前出土1件形体粗大的象牙锥形束发器，显示出其非同一般的身份地位。

崧泽文化遗存仅见少量墓葬与灰坑。灰坑3座，平面近圆形，斜壁，除垃圾坑外，还有储藏坑。H48为崧泽文化晚期灰坑，在近底部出土7件完整的陶杯和一把石犁，应是专门储藏生活与生产用具的储藏坑。墓葬有两座，都属崧泽文化晚期。均为长方形竖穴土坑墓，仰身直肢葬，头向南。从随葬品形制来看，其中M35出土的假腹杯是太湖西南该时期的典型器物，也是目前所见此类杯分布的最东限。

良渚文化遗存集中在两条河沟内及其两侧。河

发掘区场景
A view of the excavation area

出土象牙锥形束发器的马家浜文化墓葬(M40)
Tomb M40 of Majiabang culture yielding a conical-
shaped ivory hairpin

部分良渚文化玉器
Jades of Liangzhu culture

马桥文化灰坑(H92)内第一层面
器物的出土情形
Objects being unearthed
from the first-level deposits
in Ash-pit H92 of Maqiao
culture

与好川文化相似的部分良渚文化陶器
Pottery vessels of Liangzhu culture similar to their counterparts in
the Haochuan culture

部分马桥文化陶罐
Pottery jars of Maqiao culture

良渚文化彩陶罐
Painted pottery jar of Liangzhu culture

为主，器类有鼎、豆、壶、圈足盘等，其中的凿形足鼎、卵腹杯等都保留着崧泽文化风格。少数墓葬中也出有石钺与小件玉器，但未发现显贵者墓葬。良渚文化中晚期墓葬受到马桥文化时期的严重扰动，但从两件残碎玉璧分析，良渚文化中晚期的塔地聚落应较早期有更大的发展。

南北两条河沟内的堆积都有自两侧边缘逐渐向中心淤满的现象，从出土物来看，河沟是经良渚文化晚期至马桥文化时期的长期垃圾倾倒而淤平的，其中更以良渚文化晚期的堆积为主。河沟内的良渚文化堆积层出土了数量较多的玉、石、陶器及各类有机质物品。有机质物品中，灵芝、外套竹编的葫芦器等填补了良渚考古的空白。陶器中，袋足鬶光以口沿计就有60件之多，可修复的有10件，反映出此类器在当地、当时社会生活中的普遍使用。而高把豆、小圈足杯、带长喇叭形套管的玉锥形器等，都与花厅、好川出土的同类器相近。

马桥文化遗存在发掘区内分布最广，除堆积较厚的地层外，还发现了数量众多的灰坑，其中尤以井状坑最具特色。井状坑平面分圆形、方形两种，坑壁都较陡直，现保存深度大多在1.5米以上。少数坑内出有完整的印纹硬陶凹圜底罐。灰坑H92内出土的9件器物，分上、中、下三个层面，显示出延续使用和堆积的迹象。

湖州塔地遗址是太湖西南地区史前文化序列保存较完整的少数遗址之一，为研究该地区史前文化演进过程提供了丰富的实物资料。

沟均为东北—西南走向，南北对应，但中间有近10米互不贯通的间隔。上部宽约10米，最深处约2米。这两条河沟最迟在崧泽文化晚期已经出现，最初很可能是为解决聚落内部用水问题而特意开挖的引水沟，其间的间隔是供人进出的通道。良渚文化早期的墓葬埋在河沟南北两侧，墓葬再外侧是居住址。房屋基址F1位于南段河沟北侧10余米处，其生活面已遭破坏，但柱洞保存相对完好。东、西两面的墙体均为双排柱，北面墙体为单排柱。良渚早期墓葬均为长方形竖穴土坑墓，头向南。随葬品以陶器

良渚文化彩陶片
Painted pottery shard of Liangzhu culture

良渚文化漆绘陶片
Lacquer-painted pottery shard of Liangzhu culture

良渚文化陶罐上的刻划符号
Incised sign on a pottery jar of Liangzhu culture

良渚文化陶片上的刻划符号
Incised sign on a pottery shard of Liangzhu culture

In March 2004 to January 2005, the Tadi Archaeological Team jointly organized by the Zhejiang Provincial Institute of Cultural Relics and Archaeology and the Huzhou Municipal Museum carried out a rescuing excavation on the Tadi site at Qianjin Town, Huzhou County. In the excavated area of nearly 3,500 sq m, they revealed 58 tombs of the Majiabang, Songtze and Liangzhu cultures and 130 ash-pits of the Majiabang to Maqiao cultures, and brought to light more than 800 jade, stone, pottery and ivory objects.

The Majiabang culture remains include ash-pits and tombs. The ash-pits are all irregular in plan and yielded pottery vessels of the *fu* cauldron with waist fringe, ding tripod, ox-nose-shape-eared jar, *zeng* steamer, dou stemmed vessel and side-handled *he* tripod. The tombs, altogether 22, are all rectangular earthen pits, long and narrow in plan. The human skeletons point to the east and lie in a extended prone, sidewise extended, extended supine or sidewise flexed position, but funeral object occur only in four cases. A conical-shaped massive ivory hairpin was found in Tomb M40, in front of the human skull. It suggests the uncommon status of the tomb-owner.

The Songtze culture remains embrace only a few tombs and ash-pits. The latter vestiges were for rubbish heaping or thing storing. H48 must have been a storage pit of daily utensils and production implements as seven intact pottery cups and a stone plough were discovered near its bottom. The tombs belong to the late Songtze period. The false-bellied cups they

unearthed are typical of that time in the southwestern Taihu Lake area, and mark the eastern limit for the distribution of this type of cup.

The Liangzhu culture remains include cultural deposits in layers, as well as tombs, ash-pits and house-foundations. The cultural deposits are largely concentrated in the northern and southern river gulfs, which had been formed by the late Songtze and were filled up with silt and rubbish in the late Liangzhu to the Maqiao period. The gulfs yielded a number of jade and stone artifacts, pottery utensils and objects in organic material, the pocket-leg *gui* tripods alone totaling above 60 according to estimation by their rim shards, which reflects the prevalence of this type of vessel in the Tadi community during the late Liangzhu period. Among the ash-pits the more important is H8, which yielded 13 pottery vessels of the *he* tripod, jar and *ding* tripod. Some of them show cultural elements similar to those of the Haochuan culture.

The most extensively distributed on the site are the deposits of Maqiao culture. There are a large number of ash-pits, of which the most distinctive are well-shaped ones. These are circular or square in plan, straight in wall, and above 1.5 m in remaining depth. They contain mostly no objects, only a few pits yielded several pieces. For example, H92 contains nine artifacts at three levels, which is a sign of its continuous use.

Tadi is one of the rare sites where the prehistoric cultural sequence of the Taihu Lake Basin is preserved in a good condition. It provides rich material data for researching into the course of cultural evolution in this area.

河南登封

王城岗遗址考古新发现

RECENT ARCHAEOLOGICAL DISCOVERIES
ON THE WANGCHENGGANG SITE IN DENGFENG, HENAN

王城岗遗址位于河南省登封市告成镇西部,在颍河与五渡河交汇的台地上,向南眺望伏牛山余脉——箕山、大熊山和小熊山,西望中岳嵩山之少室山,地理位置十分重要。20世纪70年代末至80年代初,在此发现了河南龙山文化晚期的东西并列的两座城址,并在西城内发现夯土基址、奠基坑、青铜器残片和文字等,引起学术界的极大关注。

2002～2004年,北京大学考古文博学院与河南省文物考古研究所合作承担了中华文明探源工程预研究——登封王城岗城址及周围地区遗址聚落形态研究项目,并对王城岗遗址展开了大规模的调查、钻探和发掘。王城岗遗址东起五渡河西岸,西至八方村东部,北依王岭尖的南缘,南抵颍河北岸,遗址面积50余万平方米。该遗址的文化层平均厚2米左右,最厚处可达9米。

在王城岗遗址中部发现一座河南龙山文化晚期的大城城址,面积约30万平方米。其北城墙夯土残长370、残高0.5～1.2米。北城壕长约630、宽约10、残深3米,向东似通往五渡河。西城壕残长

王城岗遗址近景,近处是五渡河(自东向西摄)
A close view of the Wangchenggang site
(photo from east to west with the Wudu
River in the foreground)

130、宽约10、残深1.5～2米，向南似通往颍河。大城东面和南面的城墙与城壕已被毁坏。城墙夯土为平地起建，修建在生土或经平整的河南龙山文化晚期文化层上。夯土呈黄色，土质纯净且坚硬。夯层分为数层，每层厚8～30厘米。夯层表面有夯具痕迹，似是用河卵石类夯具夯砸出来的，夯窝明显。城墙夯土中的包含物较少，主要是方格纹、篮纹和细绳纹陶片。从陶片来看，其年代为河南龙山文化晚期。

大城城墙的夯土被河南龙山文化晚期层所叠压，其自身又压在河南龙山文化晚期层之上。城壕开口于河南龙山文化晚期层之下，在城壕中发现有河南龙山文化晚期的堆积。因此，我们将大城和城壕的年代初步推定为河南龙山文化晚期，即王湾三期文化晚期。

在2004年的发掘中，我们还

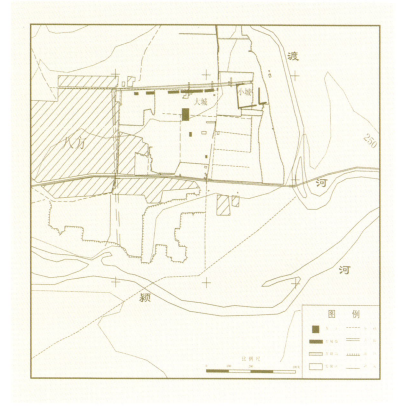

登封王城岗城址位置示意图
Schematic map of the location of the Dengfeng Wangchenggang city-site

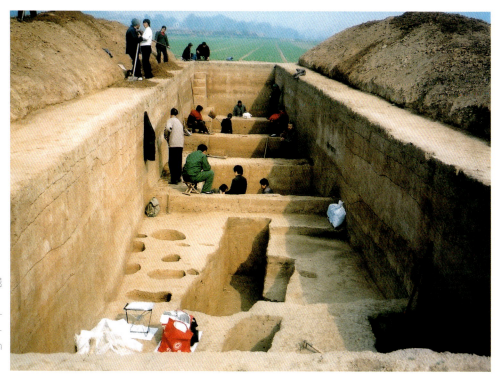

T0670～T0675发掘现场(自南向北摄)
Squares T0670—T0675 in excavation (photo from south to north)

大城北城墙夯土层(自南向北摄)
Rammed-earth courses in the northern wall of the greater city (photo from south to north)

河南龙山文化晚期奠基坑(H64)
Foundation laying pit of the late Henan Longshan culture (Ash-pit H64)

发现河南龙山文化晚期的祭祀坑、玉石琮和白陶器等。同时，在王城岗遗址中部偏北处还发现几处大面积的夯土基址。

关于王城岗小城的年代，根据夏商周断代工程中所测的^{14}C数据可知，王城岗小城(即王城岗二期)的年代为公元前22世纪。此外，王城岗三期的年代是公元前21世纪，王城岗四期的年代为公元前21世纪，王城岗五期的年代为公元前20世纪。其中王城岗三至五期的年代均已进入夏的纪年范围。关于王城岗大城的年代，我们初步将其定为河南龙山文化晚期。其确切的年代应属王城岗遗址分期中的哪一期，还有待进一步研究。

值得注意的是，王城岗大城与小城有着某种联系。从这两座城的位置来看，小城位于大城的东北部；从两座城的方向看，大城与小城的方向大体一致。两者的城墙都是用纯净的黄土夯筑而成，夯土层厚度和夯窝特征也基本相同。夯土墙的夯层之间都有细沙相隔，且夯窝较为明显。夯土墙都是用河卵石类夯具夯打而成的。

在王城岗遗址新发现的大城，是目前河南境内发现的最大的河南龙山文化晚期城址。它的发现，为王城岗城址是"禹都阳城"说提供了新材料。

The Wangchenggang site is situated in the western Gaocheng Town of Dengfeng City, Henan Province, lying on a terrace at the confluence of the Yinghe and the Wudu rivers and facing southward to Mts. Jishan, Daxiong and Xiaoxiong, all extensions of the Funiu Mountains. In the late 1970s to the early 1980s, archaeologists discovered here two late Henan Longshan culture city-sites standing side by side from west to east. In 2002 – 2004, the Archaeological and Museological College of Peking University and the Henan Provincial Institute of Cultural Relics and Archaeology jointly carried out large-scale archaeological work on the site, and discovered a large-sized city-site of the late Henan Longshan culture.

大城北城墙夯土中的河南龙山文化晚期陶片
Shards of the late Henan Longshan culture in the rammed earth of the northern wall of the greater city

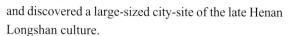

The city-site lies in the middle of the Wangchenggang site, measuring 370 m in remaining length and 0.5 – 1.2 m in remaining height for the northern city-wall. The northern section of the moat is about 630, 10 and 3 m in remaining length, width and depth respectively, and seems to have led eastward to the Wudu River; the western section, about 130, 10 and 1.5 – 2 m respectively, and may have run southward to the Yinghe River. The eastern and southern city-walls and moat sections must have been damaged judging by the lower terrain at these places. Estimated upon available data, the city-site probably occupies an area of round 300, 000 sqm. The walls of the greater city are built on the ground, upon raw soil or leveled cultural layers. The earth in them is yellow, pure and hard, and is rammed in several courses, each measuring 8 – 30 cm in thickness. The clear traces remaining on the course surface suggest that the ramming must have been done with pebbles or the like. In the rammed earth are few contents except for some pottery shards with checkers, basket impressions or fine cord marks, which date from the late Henan Longshan culture. Stratigraphically, the rammed-earth layers are sandwiched between late Henan Longshan cultural strata in the upper and lower positions, and the moat bottom also yielded deposits of late Henan Longshan culture. So the greater city can be preliminarily dated to the late stage of the culture.

It is noteworthy that there must have been certain relationship between the greater city and the lesser one at Wangchenggang. The lesser city is located to the northeast of the greater one, and the northern wall of the latter, when extended eastward, will roughly coincide with the northern wall of the western sub-city of the lesser city. The northern moat section of the greater city would defense the lesser city too when running eastward farther. Moreover, the walls of the greater and lesser cities are the same in the ramming method, and both of them were found to contain remains of the late Henan Longshan culture. The western sub-city of the lesser city is less than 10,000 sq m in area, and the eastern sub-city may have been similar in scale. Therefore, some scholars put forward objection to the idea that the lesser city must have been Yu's capital Yangcheng. The newly discovered greater city-site with an area of about 300,000 sq m will add important material data to the identification of the Wangchenggang city-site as the ruins of Yangcheng of the Xia period.

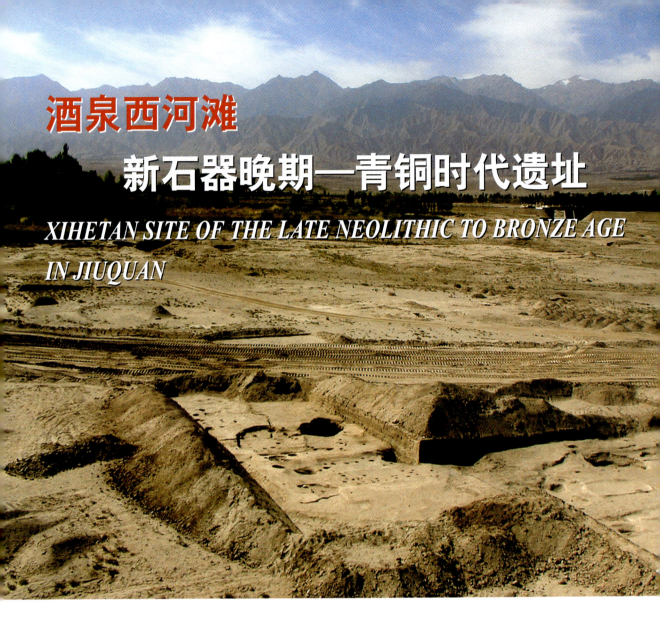

酒泉西河滩
新石器晚期—青铜时代遗址

XIHETAN SITE OF THE LATE NEOLITHIC TO BRONZE AGE IN JIUQUAN

西河滩遗址位于甘肃省酒泉市清水镇中寨村，处于一条季节性河流（自南向北流）的东岸的二阶地上。遗址面积150万平方米，其上部覆盖有厚20～50厘米的沙层。

该遗址在20世纪80年代进行的文物普查中被发现，并受到当地政府的保护。2003年和2004年，甘肃省文物考古研究所与西北大学文博学院考古系联合，先后对该遗址进行了两次考古发掘，并做了大面积的考古钻探，发现了大量的遗迹、遗物。

该遗址是一处大规模聚落遗址。遗迹主要有房屋基址、储藏坑、烧烤坑、陶窑、墓葬、牲畜圈栏等，遗物有陶器、玉石器、骨器以及小件青铜器。

房屋基址分为半地穴式和平地起建式两种。半地穴式房址平面均呈长方形，在地穴周壁内部或外围排列有疏密不等的柱洞。平地起建式房址有长方形单室，也有长方形主室附加后室及侧室的多室房屋，侧室和后室部分呈半圆形。房址的地面多经硬化处理。部分房屋保留有高30厘米左右的墙体，为木骨泥墙，并有下挖的墙基基槽。门多开于东、南方向。也有开在北面的，并在门前设有挡风墙。房屋大小不等，面积一般为20平方米左右，最大者超过100平方米，小的不足10平方米。

储藏坑平面多为圆形，建于屋内或户外。直径在0.6米左右，筒状坑，深0.6～0.8米。坑内出土陶器残片、石器、骨器和动物骨骼。有的大型储藏坑附有小型房屋建筑，可能是具有专门用途的仓储类设施。

烧烤坑的形式多样，平面形状有圆形、长方形

发掘出土的多间房屋基址
Multi-room house foundation

西河滩遗址出土的陶器,陶质以夹砂陶为主,陶色以橙褐色和灰褐陶占多数,其次是红陶及橙色陶。素面陶在陶器中的比例较大,也有一定数量的彩陶,部分彩陶施红色陶衣。均为红色或黑色单彩,纹饰有少量的篮纹、蛇纹状附加堆纹。陶器以罐类器最为常见。其中鼓腹双耳罐数量最多,其次是双耳或单耳的彩陶罐、单耳杯、四耳罐、高领罐、彩陶盆、器盖、纺轮等。

石器的出土数量也较多,多为细石器,种类有石叶、刮削器、尖状器、石核等。此外,大型石器有打制的斧、盘状器,以及磨制的刀、凿、纺轮等。骨器也有一定数量的出土,器类有针、锥、铲等。

西河滩遗址出土了与农业活动有关的石斧、石刀,以及与游牧生活有关的石叶、刮削器等细石器。结合遗址中大量的动物骨骼以及圈栏遗迹,我们初步推断,当时人们的生计方式是农业牧业兼营。从遗迹和遗物分析,西河滩遗址有四类文化因素,即马厂类型、齐家文化、四坝文化,以及以高领蛇纹罐为代表的一类文化遗存。其主体遗存应为四坝文化早期遗存。

和不规则形状等。较大的直径超过2米,一般直径为1米左右。多数口大底小,坑底又分平底和锅底形两种。坑内堆积大量的灰烬,出土有陶器残片、石器、卵石和动物骨骼,有些动物骨骼和卵石还被烧烤成黑色。

陶窑发现多座,皆分布于居址附近,以1座组合式陶窑最富有特色。在一个长2、宽1.5、深2米的长方形火膛的北面,并排设有3座窑室,西面还有1座窑室。窑室平面多呈圆形,窑室内各有2条火道。窑内出土陶器残片。

墓葬共发现3座,其中2座为长方形竖穴土坑墓,1座为椭圆形土坑墓。人骨较乱,属于迁葬或扰乱葬性质。随葬品有陶、玉、石、骨器等。

牲畜圈栏遗迹的面积在200平方米以上,周围

半地穴式房址
Semi-subterranean
house foundation

墓葬
Tomb

The Xihetan site is located at Qingshui Town in Jiuquan City, Gansu Province, on the second terrace of the eastern bank of a seasonal river. It occupies an area of 150,000 sq m and is covered by a sand layer 20－50 cm thick. Its east is now a stretch of cultivated land.

In 2003 and 2004, the Gansu Provincial Institute of Cultural Relics and Archaeology, in cooperation with the Antiquarian and Museological College of Northwest China University, carried out two seasons of extensive drilling and excavation. As shown by the results of the work, the site contains remains mainly of two periods, i.e. the Wei-Jin period and the Neolithic to Bronze Age. The latter remains are the chief deposits, spreading over the whole site, and belong to a large-scale settlement.

The vestiges discovered include a large number of house-foundations, cellars, baking pits, kiln-sites and tombs; the objects yielded fall into pottery, jades, stone implements, bronzes and bone artifacts.

The pottery is of sandy ware, principally orange-brown and grayish-brown. Plain-surfaced vessels form a large proportion, and painted ones occur in a certain number. The latter are painted in red or black, and coated with red slip in some cases. The decorative designs include basket impressions and serpent-like clay stripes attached to the vessel surface, both occurring in rare cases. In type the commonest is the jar, which falls into several varieties, such as the high-necked swell-bellied double-eared, the single-eared painted, the four-eared, and the high-necked. Among the other types are the painted basin, single-eared cup, lid and spindle whorl.

The Xihetan site has rich cultural contents, which comprise elements of four cultural complexes, i.e. the Machang type, the Qijia culture, the Siba culture, and the complex represented by high-necked serpent design jars. The excavation of the site made up the gap of settlements in the excavation and study of Siba culture remains. It has great academic significance to the comprehensive study of the origin, contents, distinctive features, periodization, production mode, life style and social structure of the Siba culture.

双耳彩陶罐
Double-eared painted
pottery jar

四耳彩陶罐
Four-eared painted pottery jar

高领腹耳陶罐
High-necked pottery jar
with loops on the belly

双耳陶罐
Double-eared pottery jar

高领双耳蛇纹陶罐
High-necked double-eared pottery jar
with serpent design

河南偃师
二里头遗址中心区

CENTRAL AREA OF THE ERLITOU SITE IN YANSHI, HENAN

自2001年起，中国社会科学院考古研究所二里头工作队在二里头遗址宫殿区外围发现了纵横交错的大路，并发现了宫城城墙。2004年春季，又在宫城以南发现了另一堵夯土墙，另外还发现了车辙、大型夯土基址和绿松石器制造作坊等重要遗存。

现已查明，宫殿区的四围均有宽10余米至20米左右的大路，四条大路的走向分别与1号、2号宫殿基址的四面围墙的方向基本一致，其围起的空间恰好是大型夯土建筑基址的集中区，面积逾10

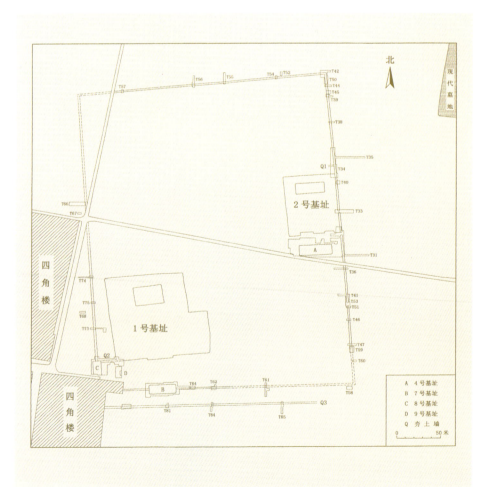

宫殿区城墙及相关遗迹
平面图

Plan of the city-walls
and related remains
in the palace area

4号基址全景
A full view of Building-foundation 4

万平方米。经解剖发掘可知，上述大路从二里头文化早期至晚期一直延续使用。

宫城平面略呈长方形，东墙方向174°（以宫殿基址止门方向为准），西墙方向174.5°，东北角呈直角。城墙沿着已探明的四条大路的内侧修筑，直接下压早期路土，在宫城外侧的早期路土上，又形成了宫城使用时期的路土。四面城墙中，东墙与北墙保存较好。东墙残长330余米，其上已发现门道2处。北墙残长约250米。东、西墙的复原长度分别为378、359米，南、北墙的复原长度分别为295、292米，宫城总面积约10.8万平方米。

宫城的东墙和北墙一般无基槽，平地起建；在西墙和南墙的部分地段，发现较浅的基槽。墙体上

宽2米左右，底部略宽，最宽逾3米。残存高度在0.1～0.75米之间。墙体夯土呈红褐色，较纯净，夯层厚薄不甚均匀，一般为8～10厘米。

在宫城的南墙西段和西墙南段，各有一座与夯墙方向一致的夯土基址，跨建于城墙的建筑轴线上，与城墙相接。其中7号基址长31.5、宽10.5～11米。8号基址在发掘区内的长度将近20米，宽9.7～10米。二者土质、土色及建筑方法等均与1号宫殿基址相同。从地层关系和出土遗物可知，宫城城墙与7号、8号两座夯土基址的始建年代应为二里头文化二、三期之交，一直延续使用至二里头文化四期晚段或稍晚。

在宫殿区南侧大路的二里头文化二期路土之

间，发现了两道大体平行的车辙痕。发掘区内车辙长5米余，且继续向东西延伸。辙沟呈凹槽状，两辙间的距离约为1米。这是迄今所知我国最早的车辙遗迹。它的发现将我国双轮车的出现时间上推至二里头文化早期。

在宫城以南发现一处绿松石废料坑，出土数千枚绿松石块粒，其中相当一部分带有切割琢磨的痕迹。该坑时代属于二里头文化四期偏晚。初步确认这里存在着一处绿松石器制造作坊遗址，范围不小于1000平方米，使用年代的上限可到二里头文化三期。

另外，2002年春，在二里头文化早期一座贵族墓中，发现1件大型绿松石龙形器。因现场技术条件有限，我们将其整体套箱起取，运回室内。

绿松石龙形器被放在墓主人骨架之上，由肩部至髋骨处。全器由2000余片各种形状的绿松石片组合而成，每片绿松石的大小仅有0.2～0.9厘米，厚度仅0.1厘米左右。绿松石原应粘嵌在某种有机

物上，其所依托的有机物已腐朽。

龙身长64.5厘米，中部最宽处4厘米。龙头置于近梯形的托座之上，托座表面由绿松石拼合出层次的图案，多处有由龙头伸出的卷曲弧线，似表现龙须或鬣的形象，另有拼嵌出圆孔的弧形纹样。龙头较托座微隆起，略呈浅浮雕状。额面中脊和鼻梁由3节实心半圆形的青、白玉柱组成，鼻端用蒜头状绿松石表示。梭形眼，以顶面弧凸的圆饼形白玉为睛。龙身呈波浪状弯曲，中部出脊线。由绿松石片组成至少12个菱形主纹，连续分布于全身。龙身近尾部渐变为圆弧隆起，尾尖内卷。

距离绿松石龙尾端3.6厘米处，还发现1件绿松石条形饰，与龙体近乎垂直。两者之间有红色漆痕相连，推测此物与龙体所依附的有机质物体原应为一体。自龙首至条形饰，总长70.2厘米。此次出土的绿松石龙形器制作之精、用量之大，在中国早期龙形象文物中十分罕见，具有极高的历史、艺术与科学价值。

7号基址与宫城南墙
Building-foundation 7 and the southern wall of the palace-city

二里头文化早期墓葬出土的斗笠状白陶器和绿松石珠
Bamboo-hat-shaped white pottery objects and turquoise beads from a tomb of the early Erlitou culture

二里头文化早期墓葬出土的玉鸟形饰、玉柄形器
Bird-shaped ornament and handle-shaped objects in jade from a tomb of the early Erlitou culture

二里头文化晚期鱼蛇纹陶盆
Fish and serpent design pottery basin of the late Erlitou culture

二里头文化晚期绿松石废料
Waste turquoise of the late Erlitou culture

二里头遗址远景
A distant view of the Erlitou site

绿松石龙头部特写
Turquoise dragon—head (detail)

二里头文化早期墓葬出土的绿松石龙形器
Dragon—shaped turquoise object of the early
Erlitou culture

Following the discovery of a crisscross network of wide roads in the central area of the Erlitou site, in 2003 − 2004, the Erlitou Archaeological Team of Institute of Archaeology, CASS, revealed remaining walls of the palace-city, and roughly clarified the limits, structure and date of the palace-city walls and roads. In addition, they brought to light wheel tracks, large-sized rammed-earth building-foundations, rammed-earth walls and a turquoise-working shop, all of great importance. The palace-city vestiges on the

Erlitou site are the earliest among the ruined buildings of this type so far confirmed in China.

In the periphery of the palace area, four wide roads were found to be above 10 m to some 20 m wide and to have functioned from the early to the late phases of the Erlitou culture. The palace-city has a sub-rectangular plan with a north-to-south major axis and was built at the turn from the second to the third phase of the culture. The city-walls are built along the inner sides of the four roads discovered. They enclose an area of about 108,000 sq m. In the southwest of the palace-city, two rammed-earth building foundations were found to be structured over the two city-walls, with the azimuths corresponding to those of the walls respectively.

On the road south of the palace area, two lines of wheel tracks were discovered to be roughly parallel to each other. Dating from the second phase of the Erlitou culture, these remains suggest that the emergence of double-wheeled vehicles can be traced to a still earlier time, i.e. to the early Erlitou culture. The workshop of turquoise artifacts discovered to be of the late Erlitou culture is the earliest in the same sort of remains recorded so far in China.

An aristocratic tomb of the early Erlitou culture in the palace area yielded a large-sized dragon-shaped turquoise object, which is a rare treasure with high historical, artistic and scientific value.

北京昌平

张营夏商时期遗址

ZHANGYING SITE OF THE XIA-SHANG PERIOD IN CHANGPING DISTRICT, BEIJING

张营遗址位于北京市昌平区南邵镇张营村东，东依孟祖河(现已干涸)，西邻东沙河，蟒山在其北。遗址地处洪积冲积扇，地势东北高而西南低。2004年3~5月，北京市文物研究所与昌平区文物管理所联合组成考古队，对张营遗址进行考古勘探和抢救性发掘，发掘面积约1300平方米。

共发现灰坑100余个，形制有圆形直壁筒状、椭圆形锅底状、圆形袋状及不规则形等。多数坑壁、底部无明显的加工痕迹，少数灰坑内有柱窝。此外发现陶窑1座，平面略呈椭圆形，窑室有2个火眼。

长方形竖穴土坑墓1座，为东西向。人骨架头东脚西，似为侧身屈肢葬。随葬品有陶器、玉石器和青铜器。陶器有折腹盆、折肩罐两种，1件折腹盆上有红色彩绘。玉石装饰品2件，有穿孔。青铜

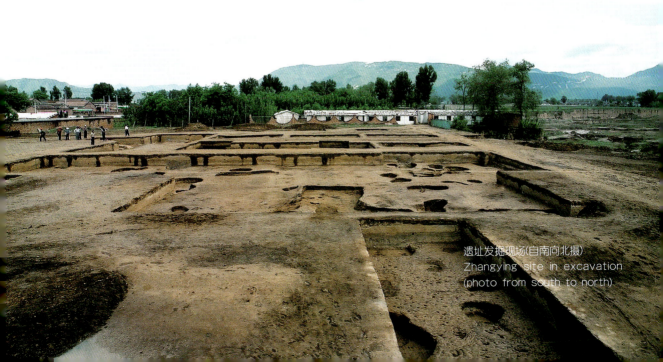

遗址发掘现场(自南向北摄)
Zhangying site in excavation
(photo from south to north)

F2(自南向北摄)
House-foundation F2 (photo from south to north)

M6(自东向西摄)
Tomb M6 (photo from east to west)

器已残，可能为饰件。

房址6座，有地面式与半地穴式两种。地面式房址平面近方形，室内均有灶、柱洞及烧烤面。如F2，有一边长0.73、高约0.1米的中心灶。在房址西南角还有一个小型壁灶，壁灶用一块较大的褐陶片铺底，形成外高内低的斜坡形。半地穴式房址以F1为例，主室平面呈葫芦形，由西南至东北形成3级踩踏台阶面。东西长2.8、南北宽2.45、深0.5~1.6米。在距底部0.25~0.5米高度的内壁，有12个横向灰孔，斜伸入墙壁。这可能是为防潮而搭建交叉树干形成的痕迹。

遗物有陶、石、骨、铜、玉器等。陶器完整或可复原者约百余件，主要器类有鬲、罐、瓮、甑、钵、盂、碗等生活用具，以及环、拍、垫、纺轮、范等工具。陶质以夹砂为主，粗砂尤甚。亦有部分掺云母者，少见泥质陶。陶色以红、褐、灰色为主，部分为红胎或灰胎的黑皮陶。纹饰以绳纹为主，弦断绳纹、绳纹抹光较为常见，素面陶所占比重亦较高。其他主要纹饰还有附加堆纹、三角划纹、蛇纹等。制法以手制为主，部分器物的口沿部位经过慢轮修整。鬲、甗等器的袋足部位多采用模制法。

石器以磨制为主，少见打制石器。种类有磨盘、棒、杵、斧、镰、刀、范、网坠等，多为生产工具。骨器主要是针、锥、镞等，用动物肢骨制成，器形规整。铜器所获不多，保存亦较差。皆为青铜铸造，种类有耳环、鱼钩、小刀、梳类器等。玉石器主要是滑石饰及绿松石饰，数量不多。值得一提

的是，在F1圆形半地穴房址中发现卜骨1枚，上有呈圆窝状的灼痕。

从出土器物观察，该遗址这一时期的考古学文化与北方地区夏家店下层文化相似。同时，部分陶器如灰陶薄胎方唇鬲、簋、假腹豆等，是中原地区夏、商之际的典型器物。但陶器群中占比重最大的鼓腹鬲、平折沿盆、高领鬲、折肩罐等，是燕山南麓夏、商时期的常见器形。可见，张营遗址虽同时受到北方(燕山以北)、中原两大文化区的影响，但仍以土著文化为主体。张营遗址出土遗物种类较多，为研究这一地区早期青铜文化的类型与谱系提供了实物资料。

陶甗
Pottery *yan* steamer

陶鬲
Pottery *li* tripod

陶瓮
Pottery urn

陶釜
Pottery *fu* cauldron

石镰
Stone sickle

石刀
Stone knife

The Zhangying site is located east of Zhangying Village of Nanshao Town in Changping District, Beijing City. In March 2004, during a course of capital construction, the Beijing Municipal Institute of Cultural Relics, in cooperation with the Changping District Office for the Preservation of Ancient Monuments, carried out here a rescuing excavation that covered an area of about 1,300 sq m.

The findings include remains of ash-pits, pottery-making kilns, tombs, house-foundations and cooking ranges, as well as numbers of pottery, stone, bone and bronze objects.

Judging from the unearthed carinate-bellied pottery basins, solid-heeled *yan* steamers, post-firing-painted vessels and bronze earrings, the aspect of the archaeological culture to that the site belongs is rather similar to that of the Lower Xiajiadian culture. On the other hand, a part of pottery, such as floral-bordered *li* tripods, *gui* food containers, false-bellied *dou* stemmed vessels and *li* tripod legs with pointed high solid heels, is typical of the Xia-Shang period in the Central Plains. But the greatest proportion of the pottery, including swell-bellied *li* tripods, basins, carinate-shouldered *li*, high-necked *li* and carinate-shouldered jars, is characteristic of the cultural complex of Xia-Shang period in the southern Mt. Yanshan foot area. So it can be concluded that the local cultural elements formed the main body of the cultural complex although the site was simultaneously under the influence of the two ancient cultural areas that were in the northern region (to the north of Mt. Yanshan) and the Central Plains respectively. Thus the Beijing area was a passage for mutual relations between the Central Plains Huaxia people and the northern ethnic groups.

The Zhangying site provided important material for further studying the types and pedigree of the early Bronze Age culture in the Southern Mt. Yanshan foot area.

山西柳林
高红商代夯土基址

SHANG PERIOD RAMMED-EARTH HOUSE-FOUNDATIONS AT GAOHONG IN LIULIN, SHANXI

柳林县位于山西省中西部的黄河东岸,地处吕梁山区,属于黄土高原丘陵区。高红村位于三川河北岸,东距柳林县城约11.5公里,西距黄河5公里。村南约1公里处的一座山梁被三川河三面环绕,当地人称"柿枣垣"。山梁顶部较平缓,地势西北高东南低,垣顶面积约4万平方米。

2004年4~11月,山西省考古研究所联合吕梁市文物局、柳林县文管所,在此进行了考古钻探和发掘。经钻探,我们在垣顶发现了20处夯土基址(其中18处分布在垣上东部低地),总建筑面积4000平方米。我们发掘了基址群中部的7号和8号夯土基址,并获得了陶器、石器、兽骨等实物资料。

7号夯土基址西临断崖,东西长46.8、南北宽11米,现存高度1米。其夯筑的基础部分要宽出台基主体,有倒梯形的基槽。台基主体采用版筑,在台基北侧边有版筑痕,宽21厘米。8号夯土基址位于7号基址北侧,东西长26、南北宽2~2.5米,现存高度约1.8米。北侧夯土的边际屈曲,可能利用土崖,稍加修整为倒梯形基槽,夯筑而成。其南侧采用版筑。

7号与8号夯土基址南北相距18米,中间有一层活动硬面相连。在7号与8号夯土之间有一道小夯土墙(23号夯土),南北向,长17.9、宽0.4、残高0.2~0.5米。其南端与7号夯土垂直相接,北端接近8号夯土。小夯土墙西侧接近7号夯土基址处,有东西等距离排列的7个长方形柱洞,长1~1.3、宽0.3~0.4、深1.2~1.4米。柱洞的坑壁及底部土质坚硬,打破活动硬面。

在小夯土墙东侧又发现一块长方形夯土(21号夯土),东西长6.5、南北宽4米,基础部分深1.3米。从平面看,它与7号、8号夯土有着共同的活动面。但其南侧一块附着于台基主体的夯土则压在硬面之上,其时代应晚于7号、8号夯土。

遗物均出自打破夯土的遗迹单位。遗物有相当数量的陶片、兽骨,还有少量的石刀、骨镞、原始瓷片、陶纺轮等。卜骨目前仅发现1件,有两处灼痕,有凿。陶器以灰陶居多。夹砂陶器有鬲、甑、罐、瓮、尊等,泥质陶器有盆、折沿或直口瓮、敞口盆、

遗址探方照(自西向东摄)
Excavation squares on the
Gaohong site (photo from
west to east)

高红遗址探方俯视
A vertical view of the ex-
cavation squares on the
Gaohong site

打掉隔梁后遗迹分布情况
Distribution of vestiges seen after the partitions were lev- eled

23号夯土墙及其以东的21号夯土(自西向东摄)
No. 23 rammed-earth wall and No. 21 rammed-earth struc- ture (photo from west to east)

罍、束颈侈口花边罐、小口折肩罐、素面小罐、杯、钵、斝等。纹饰以绳纹居多，亦有云雷纹、三角划纹、内填绳纹的三角纹、饰于鬲腹部的楔形点纹等。

为了判断夯土基址的年代，我们布下6条探沟，对打破夯土的灰坑进行发掘。灰坑内所出陶片均与高红H1的近似。在T03夯层中夹有厚约20厘米的灰土，出土少量陶片，其纹饰特征与灰坑内所出陶片相似。高红H1的年代为商代，所以，夯土基址的年代也应在商时期。

Liulin County lies on the western border of middle Shanxi, on the eastern bank of the Yellow River, with the Sanchuan River running through from east to west. On the northern bank of the Sanchuan River, there stands Gaohong Village, which is about 11.5 km west of the seat of Liulin County and 5 km east of the Jundu Ferry of the Yellow River. Situated in the Lüliang mountain area, it belongs to the hilly land of the loess plateau. To the south of the village, the Sanchuan River surrounds a ridge on three sides, and the No. 307 state-built highway extends along the northern side. This ridge is called Shizaoyuan among the natives. In terrain it is

骨锥
Bone awls

陶罍
Pottery *lei* pot

陶鬲
Pottery *li* tripod

higher in the northwest and lower in the southeast, with a fairly gentle gradient in the east and south and a steep one in the west and north. A crisscross network of gullies cuts it into several relatively separate units varying in size. From the upper to the lower slopes, pottery shards of the Shang, Warring States and Han periods were found here and there, and Ash-pit Gaohong-H2 is discovered just at this locality. The relatively level summit is also higher in the west and lower in the east, and measures about 40,000 sq m. Exploration by drilling revealed 20 plots of rammed-earth house-foundations, covering 4,000 sq m in total area. Of them 18 are distributed in the lower east, largely skirting the eastern cliff from north to south. To confirm the date and structure of these foundations, excavation was carried out on the 7th and 8th foundations. The former stands in the middle of the group of remains, with the major axis pointing to the

east and west, and is the largest in scale. The latter is to the north of Foundation 7. The unearthed objects include numbers of pottery shards and animal bones, and some stone implements and bone artifacts. Among the other finds are specimens of charcoal and soil with pollen. Some soil samples have been analyzed by flotation.

These extensive rammed earth foundations suggest that the buildings were certainly made upon collective force and the site must have been the place of a strong political group's activities. The Gaohong house-foundations and the same type of Shang period remains are distributed along the banks of the Yellow River in Shaanxi and Shanxi, and the problem of their origin has long remained unsettled. This season of drilling and excavation brought to light valuable material data and enriched our knowledge of the cultural contents of these remains.

山西浮山
桥北商周墓

SHANG AND ZHOU TOMBS AT QIAOBEI
IN FUSHAN, SHANXI

山西浮山地处太岳山南部，在临汾盆地东缘。桥北村在县城东北约7公里处，商周墓地位于村西300米处。1998年墓葬开始被盗，2001年缴获文物中，有带"先"字铭文的商代铜器。2003年3～6月，以山西省考古研究所为主的桥北考古队在此进行大规模钻探、发掘，发掘面积2600多平方米。共发掘商、西周及春秋时期墓葬31座，可分为大、中、小型三类。此外还有战国墓、汉墓各1座。

大型墓有5座(M1、M8、M9、M18、M28)，均由墓室和墓道组成，南北向。除M9为"甲"字形墓外，其余4座皆为长方形墓。M1和M18的规模较大，墓道中有随葬的殉人及车、马。

M1方向11.5°，已被盗。墓口全长24.84米，南端宽2.7、北端宽4米。距离墓道南端6.3米处有一殉人，殉人之北是马、车。殉人男性，30岁左右，俯身直肢葬，头向南，面朝下。2匹马殉于车辕两侧，相背侧卧。车辕呈南北向，通长256厘米。车厢平面呈馒头形，东西长84～114、南北宽约80、高46厘米。车厢后部设有宽40厘米的车门，车门两侧各有铜把手1件。车厢底部有大铜泡40件。车厢内有玉觿、铜镞、骨饰、弓形器、铜铃、骨器等。车轮置于车厢东西两侧，直径136厘米。墓室口长

M1墓道(自南向北摄)
Tomb-passage in
M1 (photo from
south to north)

M1 墓道内的车、马及殉人(自南向北摄)
Chariot, horses and human victim in the tomb-
passage of M1 (photo from south to north)

M20 内的牛头、殉人及殉狗情况
Ox-head and human and dog victims in M20

5.74～5.88、宽3.52～4、深9.1米。墓室内椁顶有2只殉狗,均头朝南。椁约为长方形,长3.46、宽约2.1米。椁底有一长方形腰坑,椁外为生土二层台,台上的殉人、殉狗被破坏。棺椁内大量的铜器、玉器被盗。

M9方向10°,打破M8,已被盗。为带墓道的"甲"字形墓,竖长方形,口略大于底。上口长7.96～8.06、宽2.52～2.66、深0.3～4.5米。墓室内的棺椁已被盗一空。椁室长约2.92、宽1.8、高1.4米。椁上有殉人、狗、牛头,分为两层。第一层距墓口3.8米,殉狗9条。第二层距墓口4.4米处,在东南角有一牛头,头朝南。东南有一殉人,女性,30岁以下。东北有一殉人,男性,20岁左右。西北有一殉人,男性,25岁左右。西南有一殉人,女性,25岁左右。殉人均为仰身直肢,随葬少

量的蚌饰、石璜、骨饰等。椁下有腰坑2个,1号坑殉狗,2号坑殉一成年男性。

中型墓有9座(M11、M13、M19～M24、M27),均遭盗掘。墓口长3米以上,宽多在2米以上,少数墓宽1.5米以上,墓口面积为5～7平方米。填土均经过夯打。葬具除M22～M24为一棺外,余均一棺一椁。除M24外,其余墓葬的椁底或棺底都有腰坑,腰坑内殉一狗。M13、M20、M27还有殉人。劫余的随葬品很少,主要是陶鬲和玉鹰。

小型墓有17座(M3～M7、M10、M12、M14～M17、M25、M26、M29～M32)。除M26外,其余墓葬的墓口面积均在3平方米以下。只有M14填土经过夯打。M3、M12、M26、M29、M32为一椁一棺,其余皆为单棺。

14座大、中型墓的年代上限是商代晚期,下限

陶鬲
Pottery *li* tripod

陶簋
Pottery *gui* food container

铜觚
Bronze *gu* cup

铜罍
Bronze *lei* pot

铜车軎饰
Chariot fitting in bronze

铜弓形饰
Bow-shaped bronze object

玉鹰
Jade owl

骨管
Bone tube

玉觽
Jade *xi* untying implement

不晚于西周中期。M1 和 M18 都出土了铜弓形器，这种器物在中原地区一直流行到西周早期。小型墓从商代晚期一直延续到春秋晚期偏晚阶段。

M1 等 5 座带墓道的大型墓，比山西灵石旌介 M1、M2 要高一个等级，与山东益都苏阜屯、滕州前掌大的同期墓葬规模相当。其墓主应是商王朝管辖下的方国首领。中型墓的墓主可能是王室子弟或身处要职的官员。没有铜容器的小型墓，属西周与春秋两个时期，墓主人应为庶民。

墓葬被盗铜器中，觚、罍、斝屡见带"先"字的铭文或族徽。这里是否是一处先氏(国)墓地，还有待研究。

Shanxi Fushan lies in the south of the Taiye Mountain area, on the eastern border of the Linfen Basin. Qiaobei Village is located about 7 km northeast of the seat of Fushan County, in the territory of Beiwang Township. From 1998 to 2002, tomb robbing happened repeatedly.

In March to June 2003, the Shanxi Provincial Institute of Archaeology carried out excavation in the Shang and Zhou cemetery at South Geda of Qiaobei. In the excavated area of more than 2,600 sq m they revealed 31 Shang, Western Zhou and Spring-and-Autumn periods tombs, one Warring States period grave and one Han burial. The tombs of Shang, Western Zhou and Spring-and-Autumn periods are all earthen pits and can be divided into three categories according to their size, shape and date. The first category embraces 5 large-sized tombs, consisting of chambers and passages, containing human and dog victims, and furnished with waist-pits. They are I-shaped except for " 甲 "-shaped M9. M1 and M18 are larger in size and their human victims, chariots and horses are buried in the passage. The second category comprises 9 medium-sized tombs over 3 m long for the opening and largely above 2 m wide. They also have waist-pits and human and dog victims. The third category is formed of 17 small-sized tombs measuring less than 3 sq m in the area of the opening except for M26. M3, M12, M26, M29 and M32 are furnished with a chamber and a coffin each, while the rest with single coffin in each case. The large- and medium-sized tombs have both chambers and coffins, but all of them were robbed. They date from the late Shang to the early Western Zhou; and the small-sized burial, from the late Shang through the late Spring-and-Autumn period.

The Qiaobei cemetery of the Shang period was a burial ground of a local state under the Shang Dynasty, with the five large-sized tombs built as ruler-rank graves. The unearthed bronzes, pottery vessels, jades and bone artifacts are often fine in craftsmanship, e.g. the Shang pottery *li* tripod from M22 and the local style *li* from M27. Among the bronzes yielded from robbed tombs are *gu* cups, *lei* pots and *jia* tripods with inscription or ethnic emblem "Xian 先," which might evidence that the cemetery belonged to the Xian State or Clan.

湖南宁乡黄材
炭河里西周城址

TANHELI CITY-SITE OF THE WESTERN ZHOU PERIOD
AT HUANGCAI IN NINGXIANG, HUNAN

宁乡位于湖南省中部的沩水中上游,炭河里遗址位于长沙市宁乡县黄材镇寨子村。它处在黄材盆地中央的冲积平原上,在黄材河、塅溪、胜溪三条小河交汇处的北岸,属河流一级阶地。20世纪30年代以来,在遗址附近陆续出土多件商周青铜器,如四羊方尊、人面方鼎、兽面纹瓿、癸☐卣、戈卣、云纹铙、象纹大铙等。2003年11月~2004年12月,湖南省文物考古研究所、长沙市考古研究所、宁乡县文物管理所等单位联合,对炭河里遗址进行了两次大规模发掘,发掘面积近3000平方米。

我们发现并解剖了西周时期的城墙遗迹。城墙残长200多米,宽约15米,高出地面约2米。基本呈弧形,其大部分因附近河流改道,已被冲毁。根据城墙的弧度进行圆形复原,可推知城内原有面积约20万平方米。而现存面积约2万平方米,为原面积的十分之一。

城墙的结构分为上下两部分。下部为基础部分,厚约1米,由较纯的黄色黏土略施夯打,堆筑而成。基础部分建在自然形成的砂砾层上,为防止墙体移位,当时人对砂砾层地表进行了清理,使其中间形成凹槽。基础之上是用砂砾堆筑的城墙主体。为防止主体部分滑坡,在城墙外侧用含有陶片、烧土的黏土层层夯筑,形成宽1米以上的护坡。从城墙及护坡内出土的陶片判断,城墙的建筑和使用年代为西周时期。

我们在城外发现一条壕沟,宽约6、深1米,与城墙相距12米左右。钻探显示,其走向与城墙一致。另外在城内也发现两条壕沟。其中一条壕沟距

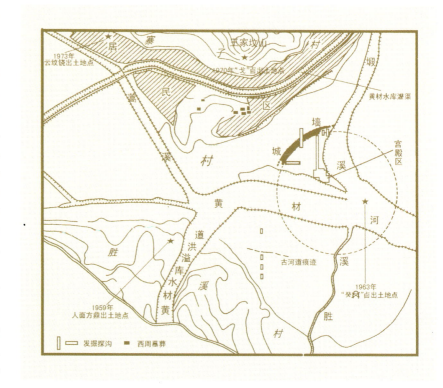

西周城址位置示意图
Schematic map of the location of the Western Zhou city-site

遗址远眺(自东南向西北摄)
A distant view of the site (photo from southeast to northwest)

城墙东北端近景(自北向南摄)
A close view of the northeastern section of the city-wall (photo from north to south)

2号人工土台建筑基址(自西
向东摄)
No. 2 man-made
earthen building-foun-
dation (photo from west
to east)

城外壕沟(自东南向西北摄)
Drain outside the city
(photo from southeast
to northwest)

离城墙约25～30米，走向与城墙方向一致。壕沟宽10米左右，其堆积可分5层，均出土了西周时期的陶片。此壕沟是修筑城墙和大型建筑台基时，在这里取土而形成的。

我们还在城址内揭露出同时存在的两座大型建筑台基。基址南北相距10余米，均为人工搬运黄土堆垒而成，方向东西向，形状长方形。1号台基（F1）位于遗址东南部，东西残长31.5、南北残宽15米，台基上有排列整齐的柱坑25个。2号台基（F2）东西残长36、南北残宽约20米，在台基上发现柱坑36个。这两座建筑基址的年代不晚于西周时期，可能是两座宫殿建筑。

在F1、F2之下还有三个时期的大型房屋遗迹。其中第3层下的F3亦是用黄土筑成地面，但厚度较薄，因大部分被F1覆盖，没有全面揭露。在F2下面的相同层位（第3层）也发现类似的黄土地面，可能是与F3同时存在的另一建筑基址。在第5层下也发现两座房屋（F4、F5），亦是与F1、F2同等规模的回廊式大型木结构建筑，不同的是，它们没有黄土台基或地面。第6层下（即生土面上）的房屋遗迹规格较低，且发

铜卣盖
Cover of a bronze *you* pot

铜鼎残片
Fragment of a bronze *ding* tripod

铜铲
Bronze spade

铜鼎残片
Fragment of a bronze *ding* tripod

铜鸮
Owl-shaped bronze *you* pot

现灶坑等生活遗迹，房址年代为商代末期。

此外，我们在城址西北的台地上清理出7座西周墓，墓主人的身份是中下层贵族。这批墓葬均为长方形竖穴土坑墓，墓口长3～3.5、宽1.3～1.8米，深度均在2米以下。随葬品以铜器和玉器为主，其中陶器与城址内出土陶器的面貌一致。

墓葬出土铜器数十件，大多为破碎的残片和部件。器类有鼎、卣、罍、爵、盉、铲、刮刀、矛等，其中鼎的数量最多。玉器200余件，主要是珠、管类，另有少量玦、鱼。玉质较软，颜色多呈鸡骨白。从整体上看，墓葬出土的铜器与在城内采集的铜器残片及以往出土的铜器类似，玉器也和城内采集的玉器及戈卣、癸⋀卣所贮玉器近同。因而我们初步认定，城址、墓葬和以往出土的青铜器同属一个文化共同体，即同属于以炭河里遗址为代表的考古学文化，年代主要是西周时期。

以炭河里遗址为代表的考古学文化不属于商周文化范畴，而是本地土著文化与受商文化影响的外来文化的高度融合。其陶器不见任何周文化的典型器类，也不见商文化的典型陶器，却见南方商代晚期常见的簋、盆、豆、罐等。从铜器来看，年代较早的基本上是商文化风格，较晚的已开始出现本地东周时期越式青铜器的特征。这说明，它是一个独立于周文化之外的地方青铜文化。

The Tanheli site is situated at Huangcai Town in Ningxiang County, Hunan Province. It was discovered and identified as a Shang-Zhou period site in 1963. In 2001, trial excavation revealed remains of a man-made earthen platform. From the late 2003 to the spring of 2004, the Hunan Provincial Institute of Cultural Relics and Archaeology carried out here a large-scale excavation, which resulted in the revelation of important data in the excavated area of more than 2,000 sq m.

Firstly, they discovered and confirmed the existence of a Western Zhou city-site. Secondly, they discovered and excavated two man-made earthen foundation-platforms. Thirdly, they excavated aristocratic tombs of the Western Zhou on a terrace northwest of the city, and brought to light plenty of bronzes and jades.

Owing to the change of nearby river-courses, the city-site has been mostly washed away. The existing city-wall looks like an arc and measures about 300 m in length, 12-15 m in width and 1 − 2 m in the height above the surrounding ground. It is known through selective excavation that the city-walls are structured by ramming and piling the earth fetched from nearby places, and were built and used in the western Zhou period. A reconstruction of the enclosure as a round according to the arc-shaped remaining wall suggests that originally the city must have occupied an area of over 200,000 sq m. The two large-sized building foundations are piled up of man-carried loess, and stands side by side in a north-to-south line with an interval of above 10 m. They are identical with each other in stratigraphic position, orientation and size, both facing to the south. The first foundation is 31.5 and 15 m in remaining length and width respectively, while the second, 36 and 20 m. On the surface are regularly-arranged post-holes but no extensive burnt clay, which suggests that they may have been large-sized timber-structured surface-buildings, perhaps palaces.

The Western Zhou tombs excavated outside the city-walls are all small-sized earthen pits, and the bronzes they yielded are largely broken, while the jades are mainly tubes and beads. Their owners might have been middle- and lower-rank aristocrats.

The significance of the findings at Tanheli can be summed up as follows: Firstly, the Western Zhou city-

陶釜
Pottery *fu* cauldron

陶鼎
Pottery *ding* tripod

site and large-sized building foundations are recorded not only for the first time in the Hunan region, but also as a rare discovery in the whole South China. It suggests that this locus was one of the central settlements of a regional culture in the Shang-Zhou period, very possibly the capital of a local state. Secondly, the city-site is located in the central area that draws great attention for the unearthed Shang-Zhou Ningxiang Bronzes. A lot of signs indicate its close relationship with this bronze assemblage. This is of great importance to the study of these bronzes.

At present the Hunan Provincial Institute of Cultural Relics and Archaeology is continuing to excavate the site and carrying out extensive survey and drilling round the ruined city so as to determine its absolute date still more definitely and find out the main cemetery related to it.

安徽霍邱
堰台西周聚落遗址

WESTERN ZHOU SETTLEMENT SITE
AT YANTAI IN HUOQIU, ANHUI

堰台遗址位于安徽省霍邱县石店镇韩店村，现存面积约4000平方米。2004年1～8月，安徽省文物考古研究所对该遗址进行了抢救性发掘，发掘面积约2900平方米。发现环壕、红烧土建筑基址以及房址、墓葬和灰坑等，出土各类文物千余件，取得了重要收获。

该遗址是一处平面略呈圆形的台子，高于周围水田约2米，是一处典型的台形遗址。遗址现地表中间略高，四周略低，呈馒头状。堰湾河紧挨遗址西侧，由西北流向东南，注入城西湖。环壕环绕遗址一周，分内外两道，外环壕西侧因河沟冲刷而未发现。壕沟宽3～7米，距地表深4～6米。壕沟底层为青灰色淤土，并有少量与遗址同时期的陶片。环绕遗址四周由上至下有3个层次的红烧土堆积，堆积并不均匀，局部较厚。

房址保存较好，形状规整的仅有F3一处。F3平面为长方形，长约6、宽约3米。东、西、南三面由3条基槽构成，基槽内有木柱痕迹。房内的地面并不是很坚硬，但明显经过多次铺垫。

值得注意的是，遗址内发现了多条基槽，长3～5、宽约0.5米。多数两条一组，平行分布，构成一个并不封闭的空间。两条基槽内往往有对称的朽木柱痕迹。根据F3我们推断，这些基槽围成的空间应该是房址。这些房子分布于遗址的边缘地带，朝东南或西南，形成一个环绕中央的村落，而中央则是公用场地。在遗址边缘地带发现有大量的螺壳和蚌壳。此外，在遗址内发现大量的单个柱洞，它们不能构成规则形状的房子，可能是窝棚之类简单建筑留下来的遗迹。

墓葬共发现近60座，一般分布在靠近房址的

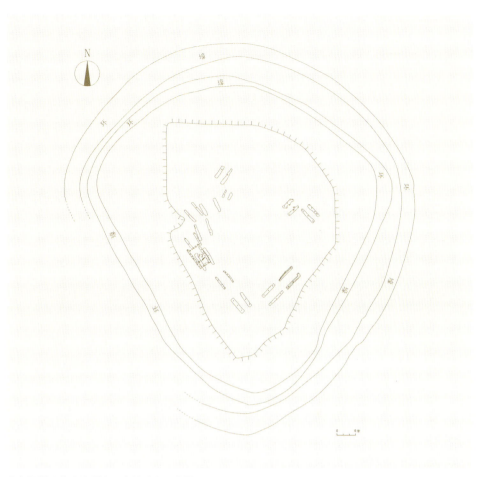

堰台西周聚落遗址环壕、房址分布示意图
Schematic map of the moats and house—foundations
on the Western Zhou Yantai settlement—site

环壕局部解剖
Selective digging
of a moat

基槽35和34构成
的房址
House-founda-
tion Ditches 35
and 34

F3(自东南向西北摄)
House-foundation F3 (photo from southeast to northwest)

M48
Tomb M48

遗址边缘地带。多数为长方形土坑竖穴，少数没有
发现墓坑。均为单人葬，儿童个体居多，少数是成
人。葬具多已不存，仅在个别墓中发现席痕或木棺
朽灰痕。一般没有随葬品，有随葬品的多为成人
墓。这些墓的墓主人大部分为非正常死亡，有的个
体没有头骨。随葬品基本是陶器，通常放置在墓坑
填土内靠近墓口处，器类为鬲、罐、豆、簋的搭配
组合。

　　出土器物十分丰富，有陶、石、骨、青铜、印
纹硬陶和原始瓷器等。石器均经磨制，有锛、斧、
镞等。陶器分为泥质陶和夹砂陶两类，颜色有红
褐、黑、灰三种。器形有鬲、罐、豆、簋、甗、盉、
钵、网坠、器盖、陶范等。纹饰以绳纹和附加堆纹
居多，豆、簋多为磨光黑陶。青铜器、印纹硬陶和
原始瓷器的数量很少，青铜器仅有锛、小刀、镞之
类小件。印纹硬陶仅见罐一种，纹饰有回纹、方格
纹、席纹等。原始瓷器仅见碗。在发掘中，我们对
动物骨骼进行了采集，发现鹿、牛、狗等动物。此

铜镞
Bronze arrowheads

陶范
Pottery mold

陶簋
Pottery *gui* food container

陶簋
Pottery *gui* food container

陶盉
Pottery *he* tripod

陶壶
Pottery pot

陶鬲
Pottery *li* tripod

外还对炭化植物进行了浮选,初步发现水稻、小麦等农作物。

　　堰台遗址的文化特征与中原西周文化基本一致,但陶器又有一定的地方特色,如带流和把的盉式盉、有3个捉手的器盖等。鬲、罐等在形态上与中原地区的西周文化也不尽相同,因此我们将其定性为具有地方特色的西周文化遗址。

　　堰台遗址是安徽省首次发掘的西周小型村落遗址,它对研究西周时期江淮地区人们的居住环境和聚落遗址布局、村落社会结构等具有重要价值。

The Yantai site is the ruins of a typical terraced settlement in the Yangtze-Huaihe valley within Anhui. In January to August 2004, the Anhui Provincial Institute of Cultural Relics and Archaeology carried out here a rescuing excavation. In the excavated area of about 2,900 sq m they revealed moats, burnt clay building-foundations, tombs and ash-pits, all important remains, and brought to light more than 1,000 cultural relics in a large variety. The excavation brought certain information on the layout of the site. In the periphery were two moats, within which houses were distributed along the border, facing to the southeast or southwest. They formed a village surrounding the center, which was a place of common use. The tombs are distributed near house-foundations. They are mostly individual burials of children and occasionally those of adults without skulls, who probably died an anomal death. Examination and comparative study of the unearthed objects suggest that the site can be assigned to an archaeological culture of the Western Zhou period with certain local features.

山东青州
西辛战国墓

XIXIN TOMB OF THE WARRING STATES PERIOD IN QINGZHOU, SHANDONG

西辛战国墓位于山东省青州市东高镇。2004年11月初至12月底，为配合地方旧公路改造工程，山东省文物考古研究所与青州市文物局联合组成考古队，对该墓进行了抢救性发掘。

该墓为一座"中"字形的大型竖穴土坑墓，封土早已不存。南北向，由南、北墓道和墓室组成。

除南墓道被现代建筑和道路占压外，整座墓已清理部分南北总长80.55米，如按照墓道坡度推算，墓葬全长约100米左右。墓壁加工平整，表面抹一层草拌泥或石灰。墓道分为内外两部分，并呈台阶状。墓室内接近二层台的填土均经过夯打，夯窝呈方格网状分布。

墓葬近景(从南向北摄)
A close view of the tomb
(photo from south to north)

木质棺椁
Wooden outer- and inner-coffin

墓葬全景(从东向西摄)
A full view of the tomb (photo from east to west)

南墓道为主墓道,斜坡状。上口宽16.2、下口宽12.5米。墓道两侧台阶有三级。在墓道底部发现10条东西向的沟槽,其用途或许与建筑石椁时运送材料有关。在南墓道靠近墓室的中间部分,又向下挖一条台阶式墓道,通向椁室底部。北墓道南北长21.75米,上口宽15.1~15.4、下口宽12.1米。在北墓道东侧靠近墓室的地方,发现了建筑遗迹,可能是用来熔炼铁汁的临时建筑。

墓室平面呈长方形,墓壁呈三级台阶状内收。墓圹上口南北长27.8、东西宽25.3米,底部南北长23.5、东西宽20.5、深3.2米。墓内填土经过夯打。椁室位于墓室中部,平面略呈长方形,南北长11.3、东西宽10.3、深8.68米,直壁平底。石椁由加工平整的大石块砌成,椁室内南北长6、东西宽5、深4.7米。石椁顶部用一层巨石覆盖,底部用大石板平铺一层。整个石椁的石板缝隙均用铁汁或铅汁浇灌,石椁底板下铺垫厚0.4米的卵石层,卵石层下填有深达3米的青膏泥。

石椁中央为木质的棺椁,因被盗扰,椁盖板和棺盖板没有保存下来。木椁用宽0.6、厚0.25米左右的枋木构成,南北长3.75、东西宽3.15、内高2.5米。木棺位于木椁中央,长2.7、宽1.9、内高0.92、板厚0.24米。棺木表面贴有一层麻布,麻

银盒
Silver box

银盘底部铭文
Inscription on the base of a silver dish

金质刀首
Gold knife-head

玉剑珌
Jade *bi* end piece of sword scabbard

玉剑璏
Jade *zhi* slotted fitting of sword scabbard

角质骰子
Antler dice

骨饰
Bone ornament

布上髹黑漆。棺板内侧则涂有一层朱砂。木椁内早年被盗一空，但在木椁东侧与石椁间的中部发现一个木质器物箱，侥幸保存完整。器物箱长1.2、宽0.4、高0.35米，出土鼎、壶、敦、钫、灶、甗等铜器，以及金质刀首、银盒、银盘、玉剑珌、玉剑璏、骨质博具、漆器等。

　　陪葬坑有5个。其中1～4号坑位于椁室西侧的二层台上，南北排列；5号坑位于南墓道北端西侧。1号坑平面呈方形，边长2.9、深1.9米。木箱内发现多种动物的骨骼。2号坑位于1号坑的南侧，长

3.95、宽3.35、深2.8米，木箱内放置漆壶、盆、盘、盒、竹质编织器、铜瑟柄、镞、角骰子等。3号坑位于2号坑南侧，南北长2.9、东西宽2.4、深1.46米，木箱内放置陶壶、漆案、盒、勺及骨饰等。4号坑被严重盗扰，随葬品的情况不明。5号坑长3.7、宽2.2、深2.8米，木箱内发现盖弓帽、车軎等铜质车构件。

　　出土文物计100余件，有陶、铜、金、银、玉、漆、骨角器等。陶器主要是壶。铜器有鼎、壶、钫、灶、釜、甗、车马器等，多属于明器，部分鎏金。

银器有盒、盘、器柄等，其中2件银盒及1件银盘皆有铭文。金器只有1件刀的环首，整体呈变形龙样，雕刻精细。此外，角质的十四面博具和成套的骨质博具都刻有数字。

该墓规模巨大，是迄今为止山东发掘的同类墓葬中最大的一座。从其总体形制来看，与同类的战国齐墓基本一致，但修筑特别考究。根据墓葬形制、建筑方式和出土器物初步判断，该墓的时代约属于战国末期，下限或许到西汉建国之际。墓主可能是齐国的贵族，甚至是齐王室成员。

"齐法化" 刀币范
"Qi Fa Hua"-inscribed knife
money molds

The Xixin tomb of Warring States period is located at Donggao Town of Qingzhou City, Shandong Province, to the west of Xixin Village. From early November to late December 2004, the archaeological team jointly organized by the Shandong Provincial Institute of Cultural Relics and Archaeology and the Qingzhou Municipal Bureau of Cultural Relics carried out a rescuing excavation of the grave.

It is a large-sized " 中 "-shaped earthen-pit tomb, the barrow has all gone for a long time. With the central axis pointing to the north and south, the tomb consists of a chamber, a northern passage and a southern one. As the southern passage is under a modern building, the excavation here was limited to the section close to the chamber and 31 m long. The whole tomb was excavated for 80.55 m in length from the north to the south, and the full-length is estimated at about 100 m.

The tomb-passages are ramps, each with three steps on both the eastern and western sides. The southern passage has ten west-to-east grooves on the bottom. The northern passage is 21.75 m long. The chamber is rectangular in plan, measuring 27.8 m from the north to the south and 25.3 m from the west to the east. Its center is furnished with an structure built of huge stones, which measures 6 m from the north to the south and 5 m from the west to the east for the interior and is reinforced by pouring melt iron or lead into the joints between stones. In the center of the stone structure are a wooden outer coffin and an inner one. The former is made of beams; its room was entirely robbed in early years except for a wooden box for funeral objects remaining in situ. In the southern passage and on the second-tier platform along the western side of the chamber, excavators found five funeral-object pits.

The tomb yielded plenty of cultural relics, numbering more than 100 pieces. They fall into pottery, bronzes, gold and silver wares, jades, lacquer, and bone and antler artifacts. Inscriptions occur on two silver boxes and one dish. In the gold-ware there is only a ring-shaped handle-head of a knife, which represents exquisitely a stylized dragon. The bone and antler chess-playing instruments are also among the distinctive articles.

This huge grave is the largest in the same type of tomb excavated so far in Shandong. Elaborate in building, it is plastered with straw-mixed clay on the wall surface, rammed on the layers of earth filling near the second-tier platform and reinforced by pouring melt iron into the joints between the stones of the interior structure. In chronology, it can preliminarily dated to the late Warring States period. The tomb-owner may have been an aristocrat of the Qi State.

四川石棉
永和战国墓地

YONGHE CEMETERY OF THE WARRING STATES PERIOD IN SHIMIAN COUNTY, SICHUAN

永和墓地位于四川省雅安市石棉县东北部，西距石棉县城约7公里，地处大渡河南岸的一级台地上。墓地所在台地南面靠山，群山环绕，其东、西、北三面环水，江水围绕台地自西向东流去。该台地高出江面约20米，总面积约2.1万平方米。

2004年5～6月，为配合水电站的建设，四川省文物考古研究院、雅安市文物管理所、石棉县文物管理所联合对该墓地进行了抢救性考古发掘。此次发掘选择在墓地的东南部和中部进行，发掘面积850平方米，共清理墓葬14座，出土各类随葬品270余件。

墓葬均为小型墓，长方形土坑竖穴，被埋于纯净的沙土之中。它们分布较为集中，而且排列整齐，坑位有序。除两座墓略呈南北向外，其他墓葬的方向为西北向和西南向。墓圹一般长2.5、宽0.8米左右，均为单人葬。大部分为仰身直肢葬，未见棺椁的痕迹。

随葬品主要包括陶、铜、铁、银器以及玉、石、骨器等，以铜器居多。陶器均被放置在人骨架头部上方，器形简单，器类主要是碗(豆)、罐、釜等。铜器主要是泡、削刀、剑、镞、带钩等，以及耳环、指环、球形饰件、长方形饰件等装饰品。铁器主要是剑、环等。此外还出土了由大量铜串珠、玛瑙珠或料珠串成的项链。

M5是这次发掘的14座墓中随葬品最为丰富的一座。长方形土坑竖穴，方向290°。长2.65、宽1米。仰身直肢葬，头向西，面朝上。该墓共出土各类随葬器物78件，其中71件为铜器。大部分随葬品放置在人骨架的上身及其头部，头部装饰用铜串珠和玛瑙珠串成的项链。其上身两侧从肩部至盆骨，主要是用大、小铜泡、球形铜饰件、长方形铜饰件以及其他铜饰件连缀起来的饰品，从其形状和位置分析，应是其衣服上的装饰品。在腰部两侧各出土铜带钩1枚，左右手臂均戴有臂褓。在胸部还发现 2 件大型铜泡，其中 1 件下面压有数枚海贝。下肢骨两侧各随葬 1 件陶纺轮。同时，在人骨架头部上方及两侧还发现有较碎的陶片，器形不明，可能是将其打碎后埋入的。

依据墓葬方向、随葬器物组合的不同，我们将该墓地的墓葬分为三种类型。第一种类型的墓葬方向为西南向，随葬品组合较完整，包括陶罐、陶碗以及铜泡、串珠等装饰品。第二种类型的墓葬方向为西北向，随葬的陶器均被打碎后埋入。其中一部分墓葬并未随葬陶器，而以铜泡、耳环、指环、串珠等装饰品为主。第三种类型的墓葬方向亦为西北向，随葬品组合较完整，主要是陶罐及部分装饰品。

永和墓地是大渡河中上游地区一处保存较好的古代墓地。该墓地出土的陶碗(豆)与岷江上游地区和滇西北地区战国中晚期墓的同类器相似，陶釜和圜底罐与川西、川东地区战国中晚期巴蜀文化墓中的同类器相似。

M5 随葬器物出土情形
Funeral objects being un-
earthed from Tomb M5

墓葬分布情形
Distribution of tombs

墓葬分布情形
Distribution of tombs

铜装饰品(如泡、手镯、指环、耳环等)与岷江上游地区和滇西北地区战国中晚期石棺葬内出土的同类器相似。据此我们推断,永和墓地的年代应在战国中晚期。

该墓地的随葬器物包含了来自金沙江流域和川西地区巴蜀文化的因素,同时,部分器物与岷江上游地区和滇西北地区的石棺葬出土的同类器相似。

据《史记》、《汉书》记载,石棉县在战国秦汉之际属于蜀郡西南的筰都。古巴蜀文化经过这一区域向南传播,而川西南地区的古代文化也经过这一区域向北传播。因此,永和墓地呈现出多种文化并存的现象。

铜镯
Bronze bracelet

铜泡
Button-shaped bronze belt ornaments

铜镞
Bronze arrowheads

蝉形铜带钩
Cicada—shaped bronze belt—hook

铜剑
Bronze sword

铜泡
Button—shaped bronze belt ornament

The Yonghe cemetery lies in the northeast of Shimian County in Ya'an City, Sichuan Province, on the first terrace on the southern bank of the Dadu River, and occupies an area of over 20,000 sq m. In May to June 2004, the Sichuan Provincial Institute of Cultural Relics and Archaeology, the Ya'an Municipal Office for the Preservation of Ancient Monuments and the Shimian County Office for the Preservation of Ancient Monuments jointly carried out here a rescuing excavation. The work resulted in the revelation of 14 tombs with over 270 funereal objects unearthed.

The tombs excavated are all rectangular earthen pits, generally about 2.5 m long and 0.8 m wide. The dead are buried largely in a extended supine position with funeral objects in bronze, pottery, iron, silver, jade, stone and bone. The pottery falls into the bowl, jar, *fu* cauldron and spindle whorl. The bronzes include swords, arrowheads, belt hooks, button-shaped ornaments, bracelets, earrings and finger-rings. The iron artifacts belong to the sword, ring, etc.

The pottery bowls (*dou*) from the cemetery are similar to those from tombs of the middle and late Warring

States period in the upper Minjiang River valley and the northwestern Yunnan area. The pottery *fu* cauldrons and round-bottomed jars resemble their counterparts in Ba-Shu culture tombs of the middle and late Warring States period in western and eastern Sichuan. The bronze ornaments, such as the button-shaped ornaments, finger-rings and earrings, share features of those from cist tombs of the middle and late Warring States period in the Jinsha River area, the upper Minjiang River valley and northwestern Yunnan. Based on these data it can be inferred that the cemetery goes back to the middle and late Warring States period.

The objects unearthed from this cemetery show a number of elements from the Ba-Shu culture in the Jinsha River valley and western Sichuan. Meanwhile, some cultural relics resemble their counterparts in the cist tombs within the upper Minjiang River valley and Yunnan. These data indicate that this area was a cultural corridor for ancient ethnic groups and featured frequent cultural exchanges. The excavation provides material data for studying the archaeological culture in the upper and middle Dadu River valley.

重庆开县
余家坝战国巴人墓地

BA PEOPLE'S CEMETERY OF THE WARRING STATES PERIOD
AT YUJIABA IN KAIXIAN COUNTY, CHONGQING CITY

余家坝地处重庆市开县渠口镇云安村,四周被群山环绕,为典型的山间盆地。墓地位于余家坝的东北部,东侧紧邻长江的支流彭溪河,墓地面积约5万平方米。2000年冬~2004年冬,山东大学东方考古研究中心在此先后展开五次大规模发掘,累计发掘面积达2万平方米,共发现战国中期至汉初墓葬200余座(其中绝大多数属于战国时期),出土了大批青铜器、陶器、铁器、玉器和漆器。

余家坝战国墓地坐落在梯田状的坡地上,墓地大体可以分为三区。在每一墓区内,墓葬排列相对密集。墓葬均为长方形土坑竖穴,以东北—西南方向和东南—西北方向为主。墓穴深浅不一。墓室面积最大者超过12平方米,最小的只有1平方米,仅可容身。绝大多数墓葬有熟土二层台。

死者大都使用木质葬具,多为一椁一棺,个别的重椁一棺或只有一棺。椁的平面形状均为Ⅱ字形,棺则为长方形,有的木棺留有髹漆痕迹。许多墓葬在葬具上涂抹青膏泥,部分墓葬在椁或棺之

余家坝墓地外景
A panoramic view of the Yujiaba cemetery

用青膏泥涂抹的棺椁
Chamber and coffin covered
with livid clay

下还发现2根方形枕木。

　　墓葬以单人为主。还有少量的双人同穴合葬墓，均为男女合葬，男右女左，男女各有自己的棺和随葬品，而共置于一个宽大的木椁之内。此外还发现一部分平行分布的墓葬，他们两两相对，间距在1米之内，墓向和头向相同，并且均为男右女左。这一类应是夫妻并穴墓葬。

　　因为酸性土壤的原因，余家坝墓地的人骨保存得不好，从保留痕迹的人骨观察，葬式均为仰身，以直肢为主，有的双手交叉于胸前或腹前。

　　余家坝墓地已出土器物1064件（套），以青铜器为主，陶器次之，还有少量的玉器、漆器、铁器等。随葬品的基本组合和摆放位置有三种情况。第一种是在棺内放置一套青铜兵器，加上铜鍪、陶豆

铜钫
Square bronze pot

铜鼎
Bronze *ding* tripod

铜壶
Bronze pot

各一件，个别较大的墓随葬两套兵器。兵器的完整组合是戈、剑、矛、钺（或斧）、削，许多兵器的木柄灰痕仍依稀可见。有的木柄还用篾条或藤条缠绕，其上再髹红漆。铜鍪和陶豆多并排置于死者脚端。兵器以巴式兵器为大宗，也有一些中原风格的青铜兵器。

第二种均使用一椁一棺，随葬品放于一侧的棺椁之间。出土相当数量的仿铜陶礼器、陶容器和漆器，较大的墓葬还出土铜鼎、钫等。陶器以鼎、敦、壶、豆、罐为主，漆器则为奁、盒一类。女性墓随葬有玉玦、石、贝质装饰品，以玉玦、珠、管最为常见。此类墓葬的墓室一般宽大且深，墓具也较讲究，属于楚式墓葬或受楚文化影响的墓葬。

第三类只随葬三四件陶器，器形以罐、壶、釜为主。随葬品有规律地置于棺内或棺外的脚端，并排放置。此类墓的特点是墓室较小、较深，葬具均为单棺，个别的在一端挖壁龛。

余家坝战国墓葬所反映的文化因素比较复杂，最具代表性的是巴文化因素。如铜剑、铜矛呈柳叶形，剑绝大多数无首，剑身及矛骹之上有虎形纹样和巴蜀文化特有的图形符号；戈的个体宽大，近阑一侧或内上有虎形花纹。此外还有相当一部分楚文化因素，如成组的仿铜陶礼器、铜鼎、陶鼎、陶壶等；拼合式的木质葬具、葬具外涂抹青膏泥以及葬具下横置枕木的做法，也是楚文化的习俗。另外，一些铜戈和铜剑也显示出中原文化的风格。墓地也见秦文化因素，如发现铜半两钱等。

余家坝战国墓地的发掘，为研究巴人的社会形态、组织结构以及巴、楚、秦之间的关系提供了实物资料。

蜀式铜戈
Shu-style bronze ge dagger-axes

巴式铜戈
Ba-style bronze ge dagger-axes

铜戈上的虎纹
Tiger design on a bronze *ge* dagger-axe

虎纹铜戈
Tiger design bronze *ge* dagger-axe

巴式铜剑
Ba—style bronze swords

铜矛
Bronze spear—heads

The Yujiaba cemetery lies at Qukou Town of Kaixian County, Chongqing City, to the west of the Pengxi River, a tributary of the Yangtze, at an elevation of above 150 m. It occupies an area of some 50,000 sq m. In the spring and winter of 2004, the Oriental Archaeological Research Center of Shandong University carried out an excavation in the cemetery, which covered an area of 7,000 sq m. With this number plus the area revealed previously, the coverage of excavations totals nearly 20,000 sq m. So far, approximately 200 tombs have been found to belong to the Ba people of the Warring States period to the early Han, and numbers of bronzes, pottery vessels, iron objects, jades and lacquered articles have been brought to light from the burial ground.

The cemetery is clearly divided into three major areas, each with densely arranged burials. These graves are all earthen pits with the major axis pointing chiefly to the northeast and southwest. Most of them are furnished with a wooden chamber and a coffin, some larger graves contain double chambers and a single coffin, and smaller burials have only a coffin. The chambers are largely shaped like "II" in plan, with two beams beneath the bottom board in some cases. The coffins are all rectangular. In a number of graves, both chambers and coffins are covered with livid clay varying in thickness.

More than a half of tombs contain funeral bronzes. There are the *ding* tripod, *mao* round-bottomed cooking vessel, pot, square pot and spoon, as well as the sword, *ge* dagger-axe, spear-head, axe, *yue* battle-axe, *xue* small knife and arrowhead. Ba-style bronze weapons occur in a large number, which constitutes a distinct feature of the cemetery. The pottery includes *dou* stemmed vessels, jars and pots. The jades are all small ornaments, such as *jue* penannular rings, rings and pendants.

The Yujiaba cemetery is an important burial ground of the Ba people in the Three Gorges area within the Yangtze River valley. It is of great significance to the all-round understanding of the history and burial custom of the late Ba community.

新疆鄯善
洋海墓地

YANGHAI CEMETERIES IN SHANSHAN, XINJIANG

鄯善县吐峪沟乡洋海夏村位于吐鲁番盆地北部的火焰山脚下，周围是广袤的戈壁沙漠。墓地位于该村西北2公里处，墓葬主要分布在相对独立的三片黄土梁上，其中西片（Ⅰ号墓地）长300、宽50米，面积1.5万平方米；东片（Ⅱ号墓地）长300、宽80米，面积2.4万平方米；南片（Ⅲ号墓地）长150、宽100米，面积1.5万平方米。除此之外，在西北部的许多类似的小梁子上，还零星分布着一些偏室墓和斜坡墓道洞室墓。2003年3～5月，新疆文物考古研究所与吐鲁番地区文物局联合，在此进行了

考古发掘，共清理、发掘墓葬509座。

洋海墓地墓葬的布局疏密相宜，井然有序。墓葬形制最早的为椭圆形竖穴周边二层台墓、长方形二层台墓，接下来是长方形竖穴墓、长方形竖穴袋状墓，最后是竖穴单偏室墓和竖穴双偏室墓。葬具中以用圆木做的尸床最有特色。木床的四条腿和横撑均用榫卯接合，上面铺排横木棍或树枝。尸骨和随葬品被放置于尸床上。除尸床外，还大量使用编织精美的草席、草编帘垫、毛毡和地毯。墓口遮盖茅草、芦苇、甘草、骆驼刺、芝麻、大麻等草本植

Ⅱ号墓地中部（自南向北摄）
Middle of the No. Ⅱ cemetery
(photo from south to north)

IM130 木质尸床、骨架和随葬品
Wooden corpse-bed, human skeleton
and grave goods in Tomb IM130

IM136 骨架和随葬品
Human skeleton and funeral
objects in Tomb IM136

系在 IM21 墓主人鞋上的铜管和铜铃
Bronze tubes and small bells tied
on the shoes of the tomb-owner
in Tomb IM21

物。在封盖好墓室后，往往放置一块或数块土坯。这些土坯个体较大，表面刻有不同的纹样，这也可能是墓志的雏形。

人骨大多保存完好，还有干尸出土。葬式早期为侧身屈肢，晚期为仰身直肢。其中有些颅骨上有人工穿孔和大面积骨折伤痕。穿孔多为正方形和圆形，边长和直径1厘米大小。在2个保存较好的人的手背上，还绘有繁缛的花纹。有一保存完好的男性干尸，头戴羊皮帽，额头上系彩色毛绦带，左、右耳戴耳环，颈下戴绿松石项链，内穿翻领彩色毛布衣，脚穿皮靴，靴帮上捆绑毛绦带，上系由铜管和铜铃组成的"胫铃"。该男子右手握着缠了铜片的短木棒，左手握木柄青铜斧，手臂旁放置木钵，一副萨满巫师的装束。

洋海墓地的出土器物非常丰富，有陶、木、青铜、石、铁、骨、角器以及海贝、草编器、皮革制

木桶
Wooden barrel

木桶
Wooden barrel

双耳陶罐
Double-eared pottery jar

立耳陶罐
Vertical-eared pottery jar

陶豆
Pottery *dou* stemmed vessel

双联陶罐
Double-bodied pottery jar

陶钵
Pottery bowl

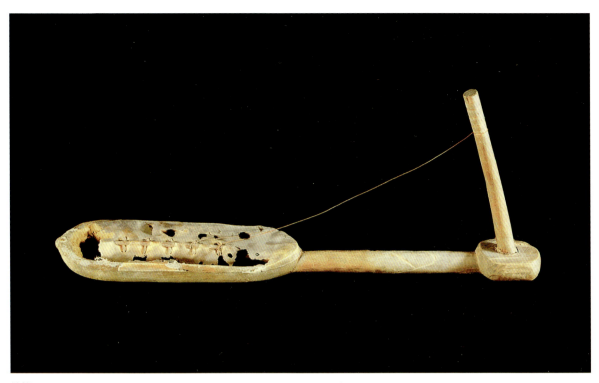

箜篌
Konghou plucked stringed instrument

品、毛织物、丝织物、棉织物和服饰等。

陶器 800 余件，种类有釜、罐、杯、壶、钵、盆、豆、双联罐等。其中彩陶近 500 件，器形和纹样都具有鲜明的地域和时代特征。彩陶纹饰最早出现的是网格纹、三角纹、锯齿纹、竖条纹，其后有涡纹、波纹、同心圆纹、羽状纹等。彩陶绝大多数为红地黑彩，也有在一件器物上用黑、白、黄三色绘成复合彩的。值得一提的是 2 件带柄陶器，其中陶钵柄端塑成野羊头像，陶豆柄上塑成公绵羊头像，形象逼真，栩栩如生。

木器、木制品有 900 余件，主要是木桶、弓箭袋上的木撑板、纺轮、曲棍、箜篌、手杖、钻木取火器、碗、钵、盘、冠饰、耳杯、鞭、镳、梳和一些木器件。大部分木桶的外口沿都刻出连续的三角纹，有些木桶的口沿外粘贴糜粒，用来显示三角纹。在木桶外壁，阴刻、线刻出成组的动物形象，种类有野山羊、马、狼、虎、狗、梅花鹿、骆驼、野猪、麋鹿、鸟等。随葬的弓均为强劲的反曲弓，做工考究。箜篌(竖琴)木制，大小不一，最小的一件通长 60 厘米，由音箱、颈、弦杆和弦组成。

铜器以环首刀、长銎斧(戚)和直銎斧最具时代特征。此外还有双孔马衔，以及装饰有铜贝、铜节

约的马辔头。马鞍除了两片式的外，还有一种"十"字形鞍，用小长方形皮块叠缝串联而成。

出土文物中还有时代较早的泥塑人头像、泥制吹风管。人头像用胶泥在短木头上塑成，具有西方人种特征。

洋海墓地的时代从青铜时代晚期延续到早期铁器时代，绝对年代为公元前 1000 年至公元前后。

管銎铜釜
Tube-socket bronze axe

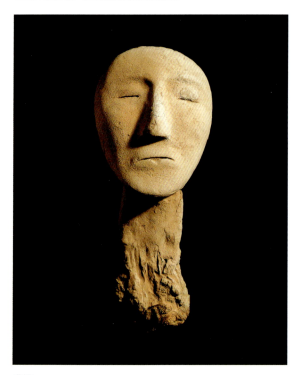

泥俑
Clay tomb-figurine

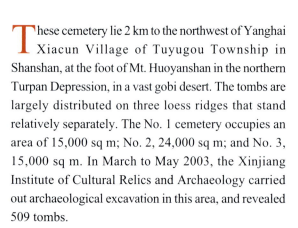

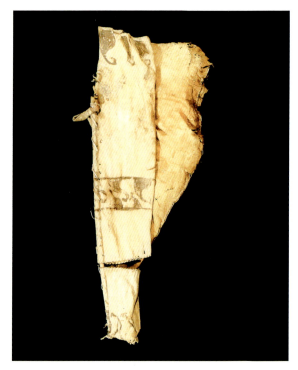

皮弓箭袋
Leather quiver

These cemetery lie 2 km to the northwest of Yanghai Xiacun Village of Tuyugou Township in Shanshan, at the foot of Mt. Huoyanshan in the northern Turpan Depression, in a vast gobi desert. The tombs are largely distributed on three loess ridges that stand relatively separately. The No. 1 cemetery occupies an area of 15,000 sq m; No. 2, 24,000 sq m; and No. 3, 15,000 sq m. In March to May 2003, the Xinjiang Institute of Cultural Relics and Archaeology carried out archaeological excavation in this area, and revealed 509 tombs.

The tombs in the Yanghai cemeteries are arranged in good order. In shape the earliest are oval or rectangular graves with second-tier platforms; next come rectangular pits; and finally, pits with single or double caves. In burial furniture, the most distinctive are log-made corpse-beds for the dead and their funeral objects. The tomb openings are covered with straw, reeds, camel thorn and other herbs. The human skeletons are largely in a good condition, even mummies were unearthed in some cases. In burial manner, there are the flexed sideward and extended supine positions for the early and late phases respectively.

The unearthed objects are very rich, including pottery, wood-ware, bronzes, stone implements, ironware, bone and antler artifacts, leather products and woolens. The pottery utensils number more than 800, and falls into the *fu* cauldron, jar, cup, pot, bowl, basin, *dou* stemmed vessel and double-bodied jar. Among them are 500 painted vessels, which show distinct regional and chronological features in shape and decoration. The wood-ware comprises over 900 pieces, including barrels, stays for quivers, spindle whorls, bent bars, *konghou* plucked stringed instruments, fire-starting implements, bowls, dishes and hat ornaments. The barrels are often decorated with connected triangles incised along the outer rim and animal designs carved on the outer wall. The bronzes include ring-head knives, long-socket axes and straight-socket ones. The saddles are compounded of two parts or shaped like a cross. The latter are made of small-sized rectangular leather pieces by sewing and stringing.

Chronologically these cemeteries can be assigned to the time from the late Bronze Age to the early Iron Age, going back roughly to the first millennium BC in absolute date.

2003 年长沙
走马楼西汉简牍

WESTERN HAN BAMBOO SLIPS UNEARTHED FROM ZOUMALOU, CHANGSHA, IN 2003

长沙走马楼街因 1996 年发现大批三国吴简而闻名于世，湖南省供销社综合楼工程便位于走马楼街的东侧。该楼基础工程的土方挖掘开始于 2003 年 9 月下旬，在此先后发现战国至明清时期的古井 10 余口。考古人员在清理编号为 J8 的古井时，发现带有墨书的残竹片。长沙市考古研究所与长沙简牍博物馆随即组成联合发掘组，对该井展开重点清理工作。发掘工作自 11 月 6 日开始，至 11 月 30 日结束。

J8 距走马－楼街 80 米，距离 1996 年出土三国吴简的 J22 的直线距离为 95 米。J8 的现存井口距地表深 10.4 米，井口至底深 2.4 米。井的形状呈圆柱体，上宽下窄，上部口径 0.88 米，圜底。填土为黑褐色，含大量的竹头木屑、竹篾、竹席残片，并夹杂少量的陶片、瓦片。简牍便夹裹在竹头木屑之中。在井底部出土 10 余件泥质灰陶汲水罐，卷唇，直颈，圆肩，平底，饰弦纹。

由于 J8 井口狭窄，不便发掘，故采用侧面揭开的办法，将井口周围 2 米之外的泥土悉数取走，并深挖超出井底。在井北面开一剖面，剥去井壁三分之一，对井内堆积整段揭取，运回室内再做细致清理。考虑到泥芯黏结紧实，我们采用水浸法，将其慢慢化淤松解，并分盛在 18 个大盆与 30 个小盆内，加注化学药剂防腐。目前清洗工作仍在进行中。

J8 出土的竹简约有万余枚，其形制主要分为三种。第一种长 46、宽 1.8～2.1 厘米，两行文书。第二种长 23、宽 1.8～2.1 厘米，两行文书。第三种长 23、宽 0.8～0.9 厘米，单行文书。目前我们已清洗出来 100 余枚简牍，根据简牍上的历朔和写简书体判断，这批简的时代为西汉武帝早期。

目前所见的走马楼汉简皆为当时的文书，绝大多数是官文书，私文书仅见一枚。官文书多为通行文种，包括下行、平行、上行文种，内容大多涉及司法案卷。下行文多是长沙国及临湘县下发给下属的指令性文书，平行文多见各县之间的往来文书，上行文主要是长沙国及郡县的下属上报的

2003 长沙走马楼西汉简牍出土地点
Locality at Changsha, Zoumalou yielding Western Han bamboo slips in 2003

8号井清理发掘现场
Well J8 being excavated

文保工作人员在细心地揭剥西汉简牍
Preservers of cultural relics being
carefully stripped the silt on unearthed slips

分盛在大盆中的井内竹木堆积物
Bamboo and wood deposits
unearthed from the well

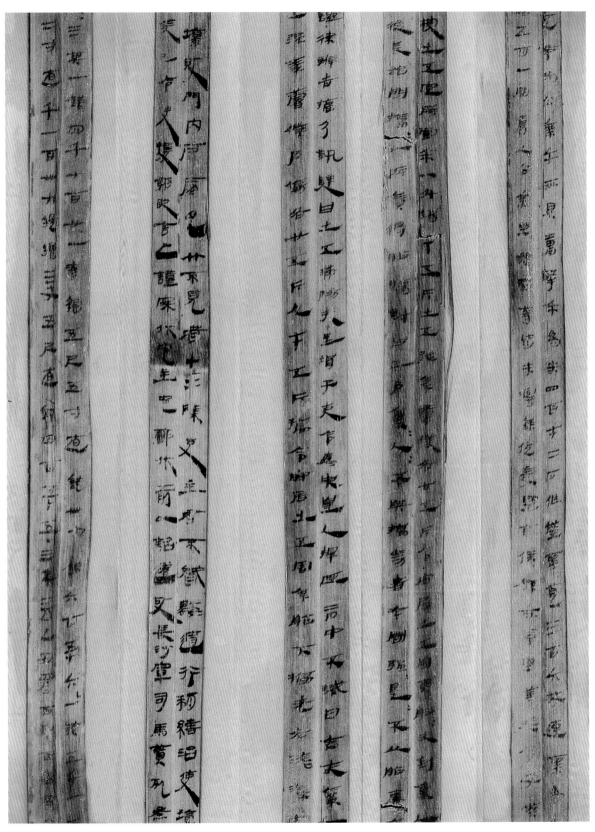

汉简局部
Details of slips

文书。通行文种的收发方涉及朝廷、长沙国，又见武陵郡、临湘、义阳等郡县地名，以及采铁、采铜等官署。

文书内容大多涉及司法事宜，展现了当时从案件发生、起诉告劾、侦察拘捕、审讯判决的全过程，其中又以有关起诉的告劾文书及验问调查的"爰书"数量最多。每简字数多在百字以上。此外还有标题简，表明在今后清理的简牍中，可能会发现其具体内容。

司法文书所见犯罪事项多涉及经济及职务犯罪，亦见一般犯罪。罪名有盗、纵火、诈钱、逃亡、纵罪人、劾不以实等。该司法文书亦可印证西汉文景时期法制改革的事实。与张家山汉简比照后可以看出，张家山汉简常见的代表西汉早期徒刑的"黥"、"斩"皆较严酷，而走马楼汉简所见徒刑表明，过去的"黥"、"斩"已被耻辱刑"髡"、鞭笞及附加刑具所替代。

有多枚简是对传舍的调查实录。从走马楼汉简可看出，当时的传舍依据不同的接待对象，设有不同规格的房屋及器具物品。此类文书对传舍的完损情况还一一作了记录，是研究汉代交通邮驿制度的珍贵史料。

2003 年长沙走马楼 J8 出土的汉简，初步考证是西汉武帝时期长沙国刘发之子刘庸(前 128 年～前 101 年)在位时的行政文书。其性质大部分属于司法文书，涉及汉代当时的诉讼制度、法制改革、统计制度、交通邮驿制度等，是继湖北荆州张家山汉简之后的又一重大发现。

Zoumalou Street in Changsha made its name for the discovery of a great number of Wu bamboo slips of the Three Kingdoms period at the locality in 1996. In November 2003, workers from the Changsha Municipal Institute of Cultural Relics and Archaeology brought to light above 10,000 fragmental bamboo slips with ink inscriptions when excavating the ancient well J8.

The well is a circular shaft and lies near J22 that yielded Wu slips of the Three Kingdoms period, only 95 m apart as the crow flies. The remaining well mouth is 10 m beneath the present ground. The well bottom, round in shape, yielded over 10 water-drawing pottery vessels of gray clay ware. The earth filling in it is blackish-brown and contains a lot of bamboo and wood bits and fragmental bamboo strips and mats, and the bamboo slips are just wrapped in them.

In form the bamboo slips from J8 fall into three types. The first type is 46 cm long and 1.8—2.1 cm wide, and bears inscriptions in two vertical lines. The second measures 23 cm in length and 1.8 — 2.1 cm in width and has two lines of inscription; and the third, 23 cm, 0.8-0.9 cm and a single line respectively.

These bamboo slips can be definitely dated to the Western Han emperor Wudi's early reign. They are administrative documents of the Changsha Princedom under the rule of Liu Fa's son Liu Yong (reigning from 128 to 101 BC). The style of calligraphy is mature official script with plain and smooth strokes. It has shacked off the archaism characteristic of the calligraphy of the early Han period and shows similarity to the style of the characters on the Han bamboo slips from Yinqueshan.

In content these documents are all administrative and judicial. It is noteworthy that they are largely concerned with judicial affairs and provide information on all the then judicial procedure, including the occurrence of cases, prosecution, investigation, arrest, trial and sentence. The greatest part comprises prosecutive and investigative documents, each slip bearing as many as above 100 characters. These finds confirm the historical records on the reform of legal institutions in the emperors Wendi and Jingdi reigns of the Western Han period; they constitute again a highly important discovery following the finding of Han slips at Zhangjiashan, and provide first hand material for studying the Han litigious system.

In addition, there are a lot of slips with records of investigating hotels. From them we see that hotels at that time had different-rank rooms and utensils to serve different-status travelers. These documents are supplementary to the information on the horse-using institution along the then postal routes known from Jiangling Zhangjiashan and Dunhuang Xuanquan slips of the Han period, and can be rated as a batch of valuable historical data for studying the Han communication and postal system.

甘肃成县
尖川西汉墓地

JIANCHUAN CEMETERY OF THE WESTERN HAN PERIOD
IN CHENGXIAN COUNTY, GANSU

尖川墓地位于成县沙坝镇尖川村东约1公里的山坡上,当地农民平整梯田时发现。2003年9月由甘肃省文物考古研究所进行了抢救性钻探、发掘,历时3个月。共钻探约1万平方米,发掘西汉早期墓葬10座,出土随葬品200余件(组)和大量的车马饰件。

墓葬形制分为"中"字形墓和长方形土坑竖穴墓两种类型。"中"字形墓为大型多室墓,墓葬总面积约70平方米,有东、西墓道。东墓道呈口大底小的台阶状,共有13级,台级宽20~45、高约20厘米。在每一级台阶上均随葬碎陶片、马牙、马头骨和牛头骨,共有牛、马头骨20余件。西墓道呈斜坡状,西端已被破坏,在西墓道近墓室处有完整的殉马3匹。墓室为长方形,面积约40平方米。葬具由椁、棺、边箱、头箱和耳室组成,其中棺、椁、边箱、耳室均由盖板、壁板、挡板和底板四部分组成。在椁底有2根垫木,顺椁方向置于墓底青膏泥的上面,垫木之间填以碎陶片和瓦片。椁底板

按垫木的宽度挖出凹槽,嵌于垫木上。壁板由大块方木垒砌,方木的外侧未加修整。盖板用大块的方木平铺排列而成。椁室内用方木垒砌出隔墙,将椁室分为南室、北室和耳室。南室主要随葬车、车马饰和部分陶器。车为单辕车,髹黑漆,保存基本完好。北椁室由棺、头箱和边箱三部分组成,墓主人便葬于北椁室的棺内。边箱上先盖以较薄的木板,然后再盖大块的椁盖板。棺为长方形,髹黑漆,外侧裹布。

头箱位于棺东部的棺、椁之间,随葬陶器和漆器。在边箱内随葬的青铜器有壶、鼎、洗等,陶器有罐、壶,漆器有盘、樽、耳杯、木梳、木篦等。耳室位于椁室的东北角,随葬大量的陶器和漆器。其中陶器有壶、罐,漆器有盘、樽、耳杯、盆等。在椁室与墓壁之间填以薄厚不等的青膏泥。

中、小型墓均为长方形竖穴土坑墓,无墓道,在墓壁和棺(或椁)之间也填以青膏泥。中型墓的葬具一般为一椁一棺,随葬有牛、羊、马头骨和蹄骨。

棺椁结构基本同于"中"字形大墓，有的棺、椁之间有门框和门。根据墓葬规模不同，随葬的牛、羊、马头骨的数量也不尽相同。随葬的羊头骨少者20多头，多者达150头左右；牛、马头骨少者1～2个，多者20多个。其他随葬品也因墓葬级别的差异而不同。一般的中型墓出土的随葬品多为漆器、陶器和个别的青铜器。最大的一座中型墓，墓室面积约32平方米，椁室分为东西两部分，在椁室盖板上随葬150多个羊头和20多个牛头骨，在椁室内有铜车马器和马头多个，在椁室内棺两侧有大量的漆器和部分青铜器，在棺内人骨左侧随葬铜剑、戈、钱币、带扣、带钩等。

小型墓一般都距地表较浅，葬具为单棺。每座墓随葬数量不等的羊头骨和蹄骨，基本不见牛、马头骨。随葬品主要有铁锛、矛和铜镞等。

尖川墓地随葬品的种类有漆器、陶器、铁器和青铜器。漆器有盆、樽、盘、壶、耳杯等种类，一般为黑底红色花纹，以勾连云气纹为主。陶器主要是罐和壶，铁器主要有锛、矛之类的生产工具和兵器。青铜器以车马饰件最多，另有鼎、瓢、镊、剑、戈、蒜头壶等。

另外，在该遗址还发现了灰坑，在灰坑中采集到炭化麦粒，这对研究我国小麦的传播途径具有重要意义。

漆耳杯
Eared lacquer cups

漆盘
Lacquered dish

漆碗
Lacquered bowl

漆樽
Lacquered *zun* cup

铜甗
Bronze *yan* steamer

铜鼎
Bronze *ding* tripod

The Jianchuan cemetery is situated on the hill-slope about 1 km east of Jianchuan Village in Shaba Town, Chengxian County. In September to November 2003, the Gansu Provincial Institute of Cultural Relics and Archaeology carried out here a rescuing excavation, and revealed 10 early Western Han tombs.

The tombs are all filled with livid clay between the chamber and the coffin, and contain oxen's, sheep's and horses' skulls and hooves. There are two types of tomb-pits: the " 中 "-shaped structure and the rectangular earthen pit. The former is represented only by one example. It is about 70 sq m in total area, and have an eastern passage and a western one. The eastern passage is shaped like a terraced pit larger at the opening and smaller at the bottom, with pottery shards, horses' teeth and skulls and oxen's skulls found on the terraces. The western passage is a ramp. At its lower end are three intact horse victims. The tomb pit itself has a rectangular plan and measures about 40 sq m in area. It is furnished with a chamber and a coffin. The chamber is piled up of and supported by beams, and partitioned into a southern room, a northern one and a side one. The southern room contains a chariot, horse-and-chariot trappings and pottery objects. The northern room consists of a coffin, a head cabinet and a side one. The tomb-owner is buried in the coffin.

The medium- and small-sized tombs are all earthen pits. The former graves are generally furnished with a chamber and a coffin each. The funeral sheep's skulls range from 20 to 150 in number; the oxen's and horses' skulls, from 1 — 2 to 20 and more. The latter burials contain a single coffin and sheep's skulls and hooves varying in number, but few skulls of oxen and horses. The funeral objects fall into lacquer, pottery, ironware and bronzes. In the lacquer are the basin, *zun* cup, dish, pot and eared cup. The pottery includes jars and pots; and the ironware, adzes and spearheads. The bronzes are largely horse-and-chariot trappings, and ding tripods, *yan* steamers, *mao* round-bottomed cooking vessel, swords, *ge* dagger-axes and pots with a garlic-bulb-shaped head also occur in a certain number. The excavation of the cemetery furnishes valuable material data to studying the history and culture of the early Western Han period in this area.

西安汉长安城
长乐宫四号建筑遗址

NO. 4 BUILDING-FOUNDATION IN THE CHANGLEGONG PALACE OF HAN CHANG'AN CITY, XI'AN

四号建筑遗址位于长乐宫遗址的西北部,在今陕西省西安市未央区。2003 年 10 月~2004 年 1 月,中国社会科学院考古研究所汉长安城工作队对其进行了考古发掘,发掘面积约 2000 平方米。分为三个发掘区。在西区清理出一眼水井和一段院墙,在中区发现一座大型地下宫殿建筑(F1),在东区发现一组半地下房子(F2)。

遗迹由院墙、主殿夯土台基及庭院、附属建筑三部分组成。在夯土台基西北角外侧,有一段东西向夯土墙,推测该墙是四号建筑遗址围墙的一部分。发掘长 8、宽 0.9、现存高 0.2~0.31 米。墙的东端折转向北。墙的北侧为廊道,南北宽 1.1 米,廊道内铺砖。廊道北侧是卵石散水,南北宽 0.7 米。

主殿夯土台基大致呈长方形,东西长 79.4、南北发掘宽 27.4 米。台基西、北部环绕廊道和散水,均用砖铺成。廊道、散水外面是庭院,庭院面铺砖。

在夯土台基的中、东部各有一处建筑,编号为 F1 和 F2。F1 位于夯土台基中部,

南北长 26.7、东西最宽 24 米。自北向南由北通道、门房、主室、南通道组成。北部通道南北长 14.7、东西最宽 4.68 米。通道北端为踏步,由东、西两组空心砖台阶组成。空心砖长 95、宽 33 厘米,表

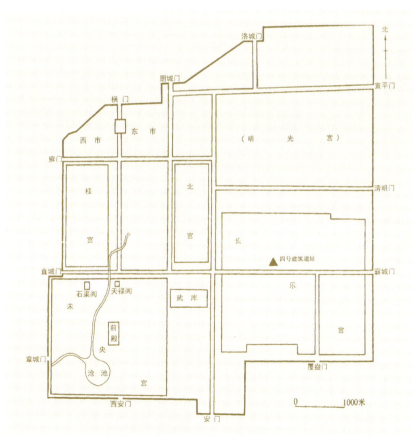

汉长安城长乐宫四号建筑遗址位置示意图
Schematic map of the location of No.4 building-foundation in the Changlegong Palace of Han Chang'an City

F1(自东向西摄)
Building-foundation
F1 (photo from
east to west)

长乐宫四号建筑遗址发掘区全景(上北下南)
A full view of the excavated area of No. 4 building-foundation
in the Changlegong Palace (photo from south to north)

面饰几何形花纹。两组台阶之间为道路,地面铺素面方砖。通道南部为道路,南北长13.75、东西宽0.95～1.88米。门房位于北部通道中段的西侧,有门与通道相连。平面呈方形,东西长3.49～3.69、南北宽3.72～3.83米。

主室位于F1的中部,呈长方形,东西长约24、南北宽约10米,四壁现存高1.18～1.44米。主室四角有角柱洞,四壁有壁柱洞。有的壁柱洞内尚存炭化的木柱灰。从灰痕看,壁柱应为圆形,部分露出于墙壁之外。壁柱洞、角柱洞下多存础石,础石

F2北通道和楼梯间(自东向西摄)
Northern passage and staircase of F2 (photo from east to west)

F1北通道东壁的一个壁柱洞,下有础石(自西向东摄)
Pilaster hole with a plinth in the eastern wall of the northern passage of F1 (photo from west to east)

F2主室与侧室(自北向南摄)
Main room and side room of F2 (photo from north to south)

F2出土的顶画残块
Fragments of ceiling paintings unearthed from F2

下有夯土础墩。在四壁内侧形成一个夯土二层台，二层台面上铺素面方砖。主室地面上自西向东整齐地分布着10排明柱础石，每排南北并列4个。础石均为花岗岩质，有的础石上面有木柱压痕。明柱础石下面也是夯土础墩，平面呈圆角方形，础墩之上铺有方砖。砖上残留一层木灰，说明F1的地面原来铺有木板。主室的南面有两条通道，底部呈斜坡状。因压于公路下，没有全部揭露。

F1的墙壁结构大致相同，均为夯土外包砌土坯，土坯外抹草泥，草泥外粉刷白灰。各壁的底部均有一排立砌方砖。各墙壁底部内侧均有一个夯土二层台，台上铺砖。多处墙壁砖的下部印有一道厚约4厘米的木灰痕，这是铺地木板留下的痕迹。

F2位于夯土台基的东部，自北向南由附室、北通道与楼梯间、主室、侧室四部分组成。附室位于F2北部，由南、北两个房子组成。其中北室平面呈长方形，四壁现存高0.23～0.68米。地面铺素面方砖，房中心有一个明柱础石。南室平面呈长方形，东西长3.54、南北宽2.89米。

北通道和楼梯间位于附室和主室之间，南北长12.75、东西宽1.15～2.3米。北通道的北部为坡道，地面铺砖或木板。南部为道路，地面铺砖。楼梯间内现存3级台阶，用土坯筑成，土坯外抹草泥，草泥外抹细泥，并刷成朱红色。

主室位于北通道南侧，由南室和北室组成，为一套间。南、北室之间有一道东西向夯土隔墙，隔墙西侧开门。北室南北长4.8、东西宽4.2米，现存高0.45～0.76米。地面原本铺砖，现存铺砖泥痕迹。南室平面呈方形，边长6.82米。四角有角柱洞，地面抹浆泥，并涂朱。此外，在南房内发现了彩绘的屋顶壁画残块，为几何花纹，颜色鲜艳。

该遗址出土遗物主要是各种建筑材料，有砖、土坯、瓦、瓦当、草泥墙皮、铁钉等，还有一枚"荆州牧印章"封泥和多枚铜钱。从这些遗物看，该建筑的时代为西汉。长乐宫四号建筑遗址的发掘，对于研究长乐宫形制布局以及西汉建筑科技具有重要价值。

F2北部的附室，为一个套间(自北向南摄)
Auxiliary chamber with an inner room in the north of F2 (photo from north to south)

氢气球空中摄影
Hydrogen balloon photography from the air

The No. 4 building-foundation of Changlegong Palace is located in the northwest of the Changlegong palace site in Han Chang'an City. In October 2003 to January 2004, the Han Chang'an City Archaeological Team, Institute of Archaeology, CASS, carried out archaeological excavation on the foundation. The ruins consist of three parts: the remaining enclosure, the rammed-earth platform of the main pavilion with a courtyard, and the vestiges of auxiliary buildings. The enclosure left over a wall section standing to the northwest of the rammed-earth platform. It extends from west to east with the eastern end turning northward, and is surfaced with square bricks on both sides of the lower part. On the northern side of the wall are a corridor and an apron.

The rammed-earth platform of the main pavilion is roughly rectangular, 79.4 m long from the west to the east and 27.4 m wide from the north to the south for the discovered part. It is skirted with corridors and aprons on the northern and western sides. In the middle and east of the platform are two buildings, subterranean and semi-subterranean respectively, numbered F1 and F2. F1 is in the middle of the platform, which measures 26.66 m in length from the north to the south for the excavated part and 24 m in maximum width from the west to the east. It consists of, from the north to the south, a passage, a gatehouse, a main room and two passages running eastward and westward respectively in the south. The remains suggest that the floor must have been paved with timber. F2 lies in the east of the platform and comprises four parts: an auxiliary room, a passage in the north, a main room, and a side room. In addition, a well and a section of round pottery drain-pipes were discovered in the west of the site.

Among the unearthed objects are Western Han bricks, tiles and other building materials, copper coins, and a clay seal with the legend "Seal of Jingzhou Governor". Besides, F2 yielded a large amount of fragments of murals, which constitute a batch of important data to studying the decorative technology of Western Han buildings.

The findings suggest that the site is of the Western Han. Judging from their layout and form, F1 must have been a more important place for handling administrative affairs, and F2 may have been the living house of an influential figure.

西安理工大学
西汉壁画墓

WESTERN HAN MURAL TOMB
IN XI'AN INSTITUTE OF TECHNOLOGY

2004 年 2 月,西安市文物保护考古所在配合西安理工大学基建工程中,发现一座西汉大型壁画墓。该墓位于西安市南郊岳家寨村西北的乐游原之上。据当地居民讲,墓上原有高大封土,20世纪六七十年代平整土地时被夷平。墓葬形制为斜坡墓道砖室墓,平面呈"甲"字形,方向185°,由墓道、耳室、甬道、墓室四部分组成。

墓道位于墓室南侧,开口呈梯形,北宽南窄。东、西两壁自开口向下有 3 级二层台,底为斜坡状。开口长 27.5 米,北宽 4.2、南宽 1.3 米,底距开口深 10.8 米。

东、西耳室位于墓道北端靠近封门处,平面均呈长方形,条砖砌壁,子母砖券顶,条砖铺地。东耳室宽 0.9、进深 1.25、顶高 0.92 米,出土"长承永福"封泥 4 块,另有小陶盆 1 件。西耳室宽 0.96、进深 3.2、顶高 0.92 米,内置漆木车马两乘,均为双辕单马,已朽成灰,仅存漆皮及铜车马饰件。甬道位于墓道与墓室之间,条砖砌壁,子母砖券顶,顶端有女儿墙。甬道内被条砖封实。

墓室为先挖一个长方形竖穴土圹,再在底部砌筑砖室。土圹平面呈长方形,开口向下有 3 级二层台,分

墓室全景
A full view of the tomb chamber

墓室内东壁射猎图
Hunting scene on the eastern wall of the tomb chamber

墓室内东壁射猎图局部
Detail of the hunting scene on the eastern wall of the tomb chamber

墓室内东壁射猎图局部
Detail of the hunt—
ing scene on the
eastern wall of the
tomb chamber

墓室内东壁射猎图局部
Detail of the hunt—
ing scene on the
eastern wall of the
tomb chamber

墓室内东壁射猎图局部
Detail of the hunting
scene on the east--
ern wall of the tomb
chamber

别与墓道内的二层台相通。砖室平面呈长方形，南北长4.6、东西宽2.08、室高2.1米。券顶两层，内层为楔形条砖，竖向对缝券顶；外层为子母砖，对缝券顶。条砖"人"字形铺地。墓室内置木棺一具，紧靠墓室的东壁和北壁，平面呈长方形。棺长2.1、宽0.6、侧板厚6厘米。墓室内出土玉眼障2、口琀1、鼻塞2、坠饰1、铜印章1件及五铢钱200多枚。

　　壁画遍及墓壁及券顶。做法为先在墓壁、券顶上刷一层白毫泥，再在之上用墨线起稿，最后填充

红、蓝、黑等颜料。在画面上有较多的初稿或修稿的墨线。壁画内容丰富，有车马出行、狩猎、宴饮、斗鸡、乐舞等生活场景，和日、月、翼龙、凤鸟、仙鹤、乘龙羽人等升仙场面。

　　南壁墓门东侧绘一龙，身躯略呈S形，全身金黄鳞片。墓门西侧绘一虎，肩生双翼。两瑞兽周围绘云气纹。

　　东壁的绘画内容以狩猎、车马出行场景为主，人物行进方向均由南向北。南端上部为一组车马出行，由三部分组成，前面二人骑马开道，中间一人

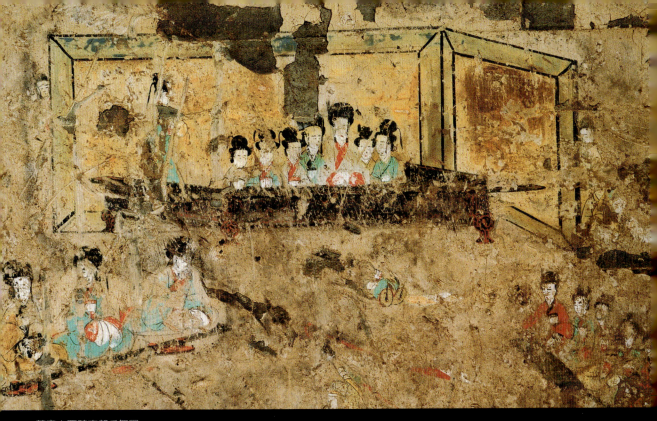

骑马引导，后面的主人乘坐二马拉的车。中部为狩猎场面，自南而北能辨识轮廓的人物形象有九组。第一组，白色奔马之上有一红衣猎人，张弓拉箭，射向前面的麋鹿。第二组，二少年并驾奇驱，似在轻松交谈。第三组，狂奔的黑马之上，一红衣猎手正拉弓射向一旁的羚羊。第四组，枣红马上有一灰衣红面猎手，正拉满弓射杀前面的猎物。第五组，一青衣猎手下马捡取猎物，身后的枣红马作回首嘶鸣状。第六组，一猎手跨下白马，左手执辔，右手握鞭，正策马飞奔。第六组，一红衣猎人徒步追逐奔逃的野猪。第七组，奔马之上一白衣猎人，手握长枪，刺杀猎物。第八组，飞奔的红马之上，一黄衣猎手回射远处的猎物。第九组，枣红马上一黄衣猎手，回射奔跑的野牛。

东壁北部偏下有一车马出行图，双辕单马。北部偏上有3个单独的人物形象，北侧人物身着黄色长袍，身体略向前倾。南侧人物身着灰色长袍，右臂微屈置于身前。第三个人物身穿黑色长袍，右手前平举，左手背于身后。

北壁上部绘一乘龙羽人，红脸膛，大耳圆眼，发上卷前飘，肩部生翼。龙青背红腹，头部被盗洞打破。之下有黄蛇和青蛇各一条。

西壁北部的图案剥落严重，当为一幅乐舞场景。中部为一幅斗鸡（斗鸭？）场面。南部为一幅宴乐场面，女主人与宾客并排踞坐于围屏之前的木榻之上，欣赏面前的乐舞。

券顶展现的是仙境天界。所有的仙禽、瑞兽均朝向墓门。南端正中为一展翅飞翔的朱雀，东西两侧各有一翼龙。东侧龙前有日，日中有金乌；西侧券顶中部有月，月中有玉兔、蟾蜍。后部券顶两侧各有一仙鹤，其间布满云气纹。

该墓是西安地区继西安交通大学壁画墓、西安曲江池壁画墓之后发现的第三座西汉壁画墓，墓葬形制与其他两座近同。其壁画内容不仅有反映墓主人灵魂升天的场景，还出现了东汉流行的车马出行、狩猎、宴乐等现世生活画面。而且画面细腻，绘画风格与同期的粗犷朴拙迥异，具有工笔重彩画的韵味。

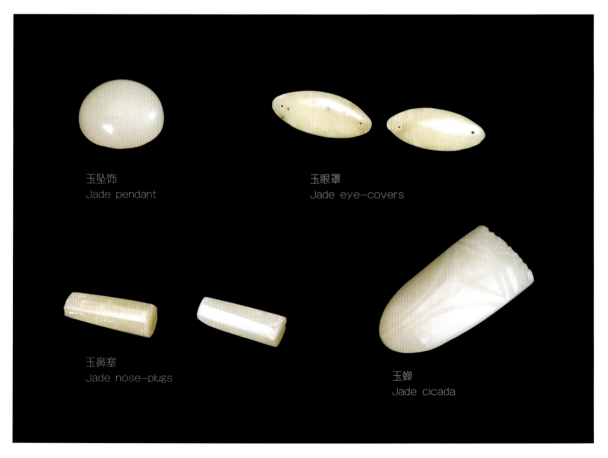

玉坠饰
Jade pendant

玉眼罩
Jade eye-covers

玉鼻塞
Jade nose-plugs

玉蝉
Jade cicada

"长承永福" 封泥打本
Impression of the "Chang Cheng Yong
Fu 长承永福 "-inscribed clay seal

五铢钱
Wuzhu coins

In February 2004, the Xi'an Municipal Institute of Cultural Relics Preservation and Archaeology discovered a large-sized Western Han mural tomb in concert with the second capital construction of Xi'an Institute of Technology. This is a brick-chambered grave with a ramping passage, looking like the character "甲 " in plan, and has an azimuth of 185°. The whole tomb consists of a passage, two side rooms, a corridor and a chamber. The passage is located on the southern side of the chamber and has a ramping floor. The tomb opening measures 27.5 m in length, 4.2 and 1.3 m in width for the northern and southern sides respectively, and 10.8 m above the tomb bottom.

The side rooms are at the northern end of the passage, close to the tomb sealer. The eastern room is rectangular in plan, has a vault, and measures 0.9 m in width and 1.25 m in depth from the frontal wall to the back. It yielded four clay seals inscribed with "Chang Cheng Yong Fu 长承永福 " and a small pottery basin. The brick-paved floor bears traces of straw mats. The western room also has a rectangular plan, measuring 0.96 m in width and 3.2 m in depth. It contains two horse-drawn lacquered wooden carriages arranged one behind another. Both are double-pole and single-horse vehicles and rotted away. Only lacquer peelings and horse-and-carriage trappings in bronze remain in situ. Between the passage and the chamber is a corridor, which is covered by a vault topped with parapets and filled with long narrow bricks.

The chamber is built of brick in a rectangular pit. It has also a rectangular plan, two layers of vaults, and a floor paved with long narrow bricks in zigzag patterns. Its dimensions are 4.6 m long from the north to the south, 2.08 m wide from the west to the east, and 2.1 m in height. In the northeast is a wooden coffin, measuring 2.1 m in length and 0.6 m in width. The unearthed objects include two jade eye-covers, a mouth-piece, two nose-plugs and a pendant, a bronze seal, and *wuzhu* coins.

The chamber walls and vault are all covered with murals painted in red, blue and black on a white clay background. Rich in content, they represent horse and carriage processions, hunting, feasts, cock fights, music playing, dancing and other daily scenes, as well as the sun, the moon, winged dragons, phoenixes, cranes, winged human beings soaring into the sky on dragon-back, and other sights of going up into immorality.

Judging from its shape, structure and funeral objects, the tomb can be dated to the late Western Han. Among the mural subjects are immorality attaining, as well as hunting, banqueting and music playing, representations prevailing from the middle Eastern Han. In painting style, the murals feature exquisiteness in composition, fineness in line drawing and delicacy in the representation of human appearance, showing the character of realistic paintings in rich colors. In short, the discovery of the tomb provides valuable data for studying social life, mourning customs and art of painting in the Han period.

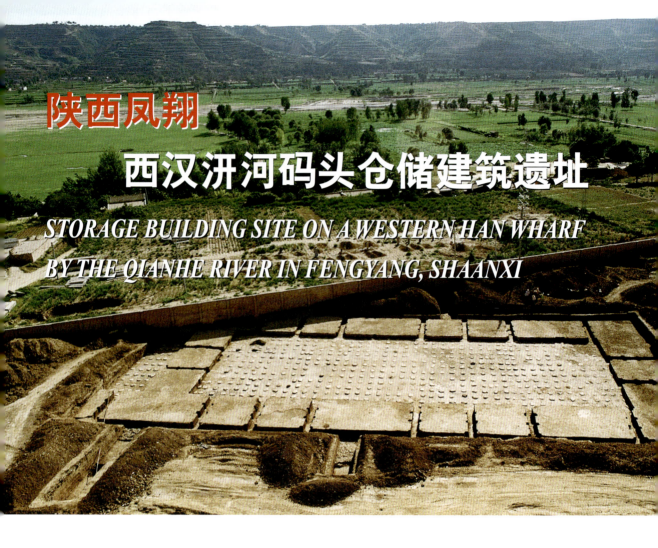

陕西凤翔
西汉汧河码头仓储建筑遗址

STORAGE BUILDING SITE ON A WESTERN HAN WHARF
BY THE QIANHE RIVER IN FENGYANG, SHAANXI

2004年3～8月，陕西省考古研究所与宝鸡市考古研究所联合组队，在凤翔县城西南15公里处，发掘了一座西汉时期大型码头仓储建筑遗址。该遗址位于长青乡孙家南头村，在汧河东岸的一级台地上，距现今河道300米。遗址东600米处的高台上，即是著名的蕲年宫遗址。遗址东南约700米处，是古代关中西部东西陆路交通的必经之地——马道口。

该建筑遗址平面呈长方形，南北方向，南北长216、东西宽33米，总建筑面积7200平方米。整个建筑不但规模大，而且构筑工艺复杂，现发现有墙垣、通风道、门、柱础石等遗迹。南北围墙之间又有两道隔墙，将整个建筑等分成三个单元。其中北单元已遭破坏，现仅存中间和南侧两个单元。

目前已发掘完成的是中间的一个单元和南、北两道隔墙，该单元南北长72、东西宽33米，仅残余墙基部分。墙基被通风道分割成18块，长度5～11米不等，宽均为5.7米，残留高度0.6～0.8米。

墙基系平板层状夯筑而成，夯土层厚8～12厘米不等。墙内侧壁均有一层火烧痕迹，当为防潮处理工艺。

墙基间的通风道共计18条，其中南北各2条，东西各7条。通风道的长度等同墙体宽度，宽0.7～0.8米不等。每个通风道两侧面各有4条柱槽。两端的柱槽均为方形；中部的柱槽为方形或圆形，以圆形居多。柱槽宽0.3～0.5米，底部均有础石。所有通风道的底部均有一层较厚的踩踏面。

墙基以内为夯筑的地面，低于墙基0.6～0.8米，夯土厚度0.4～0.5米。南北长50.6、东西宽17.2米。地面上整齐有序地排列着柱础石，其中小柱础石东西横14行，南北纵43行，共602个。础石大都经过修凿，上有一个平整面。另外在小柱础石中，又有南北9行形体略大的柱础石，每行东西2个，相距约7.2米。

在多处础石上和地平面发现圆木烧过的木炭痕迹，直径约25厘米，残高一般为20～30、最高70

考古工作现场
Site of archaeological work

残留的仓储建筑墙基
Wall-foundation of the
storage building

厘米。反映出础石上原曾竖立有圆木。小柱础石用来放置较低矮的竖立圆木,然后在圆木之上架空木板,形成仓储的地面。这样既解决了因河边和原始地层所带来的潮湿问题,同时密集的立柱又能够承载更多的重物。两行大础石不但间距较大,而且距东西两边的墙基距离也较远,础石上的立柱应为建筑中部高屋顶的支柱。以此可以判定,整体建筑屋顶为歇山式。

在建筑基址堆积层上,清理出厚 28 厘米左右的一层瓦片堆积,出土了大量的建筑遗物,主要是粗绳纹板瓦、筒瓦及云纹瓦当、"长生未央"瓦当等。同时还有少量货布、货泉、布泉、五铢钱、"大泉五十"等铜钱,以及铁铲、铁斧、铁铧、铜镞等文物。

在发掘过程中还发现有炭化的谷物，由此推测，该仓储曾存放过粮食。根据地层和出土器物判断，该建筑基址的时代为西汉时期。

关于该仓储建筑的用途，发掘者提出了几点推测：(1)是西汉中央政府设在关中西部的一个水上转运站，其目的是将在这一带征集的粮食运抵长安。(2)该仓储建筑基址以东600米处的高台即是著名的"蕲年宫"遗址，推测它当时专为"蕲年宫"而建。从战国晚期至西汉中期，"蕲年宫"作为秦雍城故都的象征，在当时具有很大的影响，西汉的多位皇帝每年的郊祀活动均在这里。该仓储可能是存放祭具和各地助祭物资的地方。(3)是一处军事物资库。在某种特定环境下，它可能同时具有仓储转运、存储和军需守备多重作用。

该仓储建筑基址结构完整，是继陕西华县西汉京师仓、河南洛阳东汉函谷关仓库建筑遗址之后又一次重要发现，为研究西汉漕运与河岸码头仓库情况提供了实物资料。

西汉仓储建筑结构复原示意图
Schematic drawing of the reconstructed structure of the Western Han storage building

"长生未央"瓦当
"Chang Sheng Wei Yang
长生未央"-inscribed
tile-end

云纹瓦当
Cloud design tile-end

板瓦
Flat tile

筒瓦
Cylindrical tile

铺地方砖
Square bricks for pavement

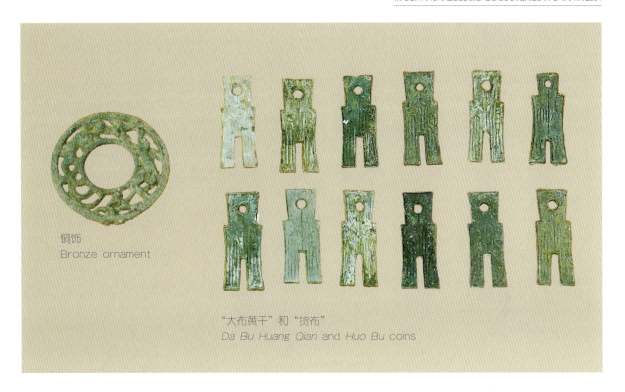

铜饰
Bronze ornament

"大布黄千"和"货布"
Da Bu Huang Qian and *Huo Bu* coins

In March to August 2004, the Shaanxi Provincial Institute of Archaeology in cooperation with the Baoji Municipal Institute of Archaeology excavated the storage building site of Western Han period by the Qianhe River, 15 km southwest of the seat of Fengyang County.

The site is situated on the first terrace on the eastern bank of the Qianhe River. It has a rectangular plan, measuring 216 m in length from the north to the south and 33 m in width from the west to the east and occupying an area of 7,200 sq m. On the site, debris is densely scattered over the building foundations. The whole building is equally divided into three units arranged from north to south. Its remains include walls, ventilators, doors and plinths. The excavated middle unit and northern and southern partitions reflect the structure of the whole building. The remaining wall-foundations are built of earth with the shutter-ramming technique, with the inner surface baked for damp proofing. In the foundations excavation revealed 18 ventilating ways. On the rammed-earth floor, numerous plinths remain in good order. Of them the smaller ones number 620. They support erected low logs, which were used as the stilts of the aboveground floor of the storeroom. The larger plinths total 18. They support the high columns of the central roof, thus the whole roof is structured in the Chinese hip-and-gable style. The site yielded quantities of objects, such as flat- and cylindrical-tiles, geometric pattern square bricks and tile-ends, and a small number of copper coins, bronze arrowheads and iron implements.

The building dates from the Western Han period and may have been the "Enormous Granary." Its function was similar to that of the Huacang Granary east of Chang'an, i.e. to ensure the transportation of grain from the western Guanzhong region to Chang'an by the waterway of Qianhe and Weihe rivers. Meanwhile, it must have had other uses, such as transporting and storing military supplies or other goods and materials under specified conditions. With the original structure well preserved, the site furnishes important data to researching into the political, economic and military circumstances of the then western Guanzhong region, studying grain transport to the capital by the Qianhe River, and investigating the storage of wharves along the river. Furthermore, the large scale and complex technology of the building, especially the densely arranged remaining stone plinths, provide material evidence for understanding architectural art in the Western Han period.

天津蓟县

小毛庄东汉画像石墓

PICTORIAL-STONE TOMBS OF THE EASTERN HAN PERIOD AT XIAOMAOZHUANG IN JIXIAN COUNTY, TIANJIN

蓟县小毛庄墓群属县级文物保护单位。1991年和2002年，天津市文物考古部门先后两次在此进行大规模的考古发掘，共发掘汉代至明清时期墓葬160余座，出土了大量文物。

2004年5月下旬，为配合基本建设工程，天津市文化遗产保护中心对蓟县小毛庄墓群进行了第三次考古发掘。此次发掘地点位于小毛庄墓群的北部，共发现10座古代墓葬，东汉砖石混合结构画像石墓即是其中的一座，为天津地区首次发现。

该墓南北全长22.8米，墓室东西最宽处8.6米，方向正南北。整座墓由长斜坡墓道、甬道、前室、中室、后室和4个侧室构成，在后室的东壁还有砖、石搭砌的壁龛一个。墓壁用灰砖垒砌，三横一竖砌法，砖长33、宽16、厚5厘米。在墓室的墓

画像石墓全景
A full view of the tomb

第三道墓门(自南向北摄)
Third tomb-gate
(photo from south to
north)

中室墓门(自北向南摄)
Site of archaeological work
(photo from north to south)

壁上还见有白色涂料。墓底用3层灰砖作"人"字形铺砌，据残存墓顶可知，墓顶起券。

在前、中、后三室的入口处均有较短的甬道，和甬道相连处有石质墓门连接，前室和后室墓门还有对开的门扉。在门楣、立柱、门扉的内外两侧均刻有图案，主要是四神、日月、瑞禽、瑞兽、人物内容。图案由线刻和减地浮雕两种手法刻成，并在细部涂有红、黑、黄色颜料。该墓画像石的制作工序是先用墨线起底稿，然后由雕工按照墨线所绘的底稿凿刻，最后在其上用颜料表示出人物的衣领、袖口、眼、口、鼻，以及动物的羽毛、翅膀等细节。

三座石质墓门上的画像石是这次考古的重要发现。第一道墓门门楣的南北两侧刻有一组瑞禽和瑞兽，门楣的内顶部刻有展翅飞翔的神鸟，从门楣南北两侧石刻图案一正一反可知，这是当时工匠设计失误所致。对开的门扉上刻有朱雀、铺首衔环和瑞兽图案。两立柱的北侧分别刻有青龙和白虎图案。两立柱内侧上部分别刻有日轮、月轮图案。其中日轮内刻三足乌、走兽，月轮内刻蟾蜍、玉兔。

第二道墓门门楣的南北两侧也刻有一组仙

门吏及瑞兽图案
Figures of attendant and
auspicious animal

门吏及马、鱼图案
Figures of attendant,
horse and fish

兽图案，内顶部刻有象征日、月的图案，其内也刻有三足乌、瑞兽和蟾蜍、玉兔。墓门立柱内侧刻有反映墓主人家居生活题材的图案。其中左立柱刻男主人，南向坐，仆人跪持酒器侍奉；右立柱刻女主人，北向立，男仆人持茶器进奉。在男、女主人的下面分别刻有一匹骏马，两立柱北侧刻有门吏。

第三道墓门门楣的南北两侧刻有瑞禽、瑞兽等动物图案，门扉上刻有朱雀、瑞兽和铺首衔环。东立柱南侧刻有玄武，西立柱北侧刻4个祥瑞动物。在两立柱内侧，东边刻有独角兽，西边刻有高冠神鸟。

该墓所有的墓室都遭到了不同程度的破坏，墓室内填满了碎砖和土。在前室的墓葬填土中还出土宋代钱币，说明墓葬很早以来就遭到盗扰。墓室中未发现棺椁，在前室发现一块随意丢弃的人髋骨，经鉴定，为一年龄在45岁左右的中年男性。

墓葬内的出土文物绝大部分是陶器残片，残损严重。已修复30余件，包括日用陶器和模型明器两大类，有陶壶、盘、单把罐、双系罐、盘口罐、三足盘、盆、鼎、奁、方案、圆案、斗、魁，以及陶灯、人物俑、鸡、猪、仓、楼、灶等。此外还出有五铢钱、漆器残片等。据墓葬形制与出土文物判断，该墓的年代应为东汉中晚期。

日轮图案(内有三足乌、走兽)
Figures of the sun with a three-
leg bird and a beast in the circle

白虎图案拓片
Rubbing of the White Tiger

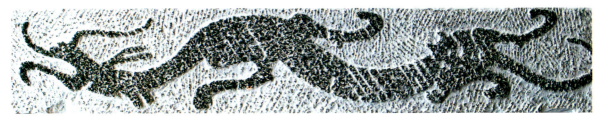

青龙图案拓片
Rubbing of the Green Dragon

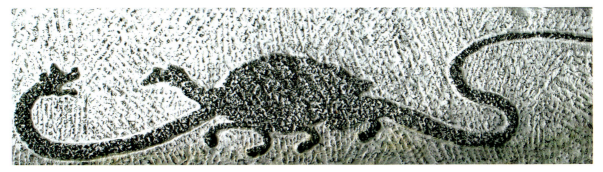

玄武图案拓片
Rubbing of the Somber Warrior

第一道墓门门楣拓片
Rubbing of the lintel of the first tomb-gate

In May to September 2004, the Tianjin Municipal Center for the Preservation of Cultural Heritage carried out the third archaeological excavation in the Xiaomaozhuang cemetery, a county-protected monument. They revealed 10 ancient tombs, among which the most important is an Eastern Han pictorial-stone tomb.

This grave is built of brick and stone, measures 22.8 m in total length, and consists of a passage, corridors, front, middle and rear rooms, and four side rooms. The front, middle and back rooms are each furnished with a short corridor, which has a stone gate at the entrance, with the gates of front and back rooms having double door-leaves each. The lintels, columns and both sides of the door-leaves are all carved with designs, which represent the sun, the moon, the four spirits, symbols of prosperity, evil spirits exorcising creatures, daily life and processions. The carving techniques are engraving and relief, with details shown by red- black- and

出土陶器
Pottery vessels

yellow-painting .

The tomb was badly robbed. The Song period coins unearthed from the earth filling indicate that robbing and damage took place as early as the Song period. Despite these misfortunes, the tomb still yielded *wuzhu* coins, pottery tomb-figurines and utensils of the lamp, box, jar, *ding* tripod and other types, models of granary and table, poultry bones and fragments of lacquered articles, from which above 30 cultural relics have been restored.

Han pictorial-stone tombs are distributed mainly in the southern Shandong, southern Henan and northern Shaanxi. The multi-room stone-and-brick pictorial tomb of the Eastern Han at Xiaomaozhuang is among the first discoveries in the archaeology of Han period across these areas. It made up a gap in the Han archaeology of this region, provided valuable material data for studying Han period pictorial stones and researching into the ideology, culture and art of that time, and has high historical, artistic and scientific significance.

陶俑
Pottery tome-figurines

西安北周康业墓

KANG YE TOMB OF THE NORTHERN ZHOU PERIOD IN XI'AN

2004年4月，西安市文物保护考古所在西安市北郊炕底寨村西北发现一座北周时期的粟特人墓葬。该墓出土围屏石榻一具，线刻图案精美，内容丰富。墓主名业，字元基，是康居国王的后裔。

康业墓南距北周安伽墓150米，西距北周的都城——长安城约3500米，东距北周史君墓约2000米。该墓为斜坡墓道穹隆顶土洞墓，方向179°，由墓道、甬道和墓室三部分组成。墓道位于墓室南侧，因遭破坏，其长度及结构不详。底呈斜坡状，推测应有天井。宽1.58米，底距开口深7.9米。甬道平面略呈梯形，北宽南窄，长2.16、南宽1.42～1.5米，顶塌毁，高度不详。

墓室为穹隆顶土洞，平面近方形。边长3.3～3.4、壁高1.6米。顶已坍塌，高度不详。在墓室近甬道口处发现墓志一方。在室内北侧中部紧靠北壁，有围屏石榻一具。墓志与石榻之间有一层草木灰，当与葬俗有关。石榻之上置骨架一副，保存完好。仰身直肢，头向西，面朝上。骨架之上有数层

丝绸痕迹，腰部出土有铜带扣及腰带饰件。在甬道、墓壁均发现壁画，每壁有4幅画面。其做法是直接在壁上涂一层白灰，再在其上绘画。因被淤实，壁画保存极差。

康业墓墓葬形制
A view of the Kang Ye tomb

康业墓位置示意图
Schematic map of the location of the Kang Ye tomb

封门有两道。第一道门位于甬道口处,用砖竖置错缝平砌,砖面饰绳纹。宽1.58、残高0.35米。第二道为石门,在甬道之内。线刻主要分布在石门的门楣和门框上。门楣正中刻一兽面纹,左侧有一青龙,右侧刻一朱雀。门框顶端各立一凤鸟,之下各有一守门人物。门扉上有3排(每排5个)门钉,门钉表面贴金。

围屏石榻为青石质,由围屏、榻板和榻腿构成。围屏由4块长方形石板组成,其中东西两侧各一块,长93.5、高82、厚7~8.5厘米;北面2块,长106~111、高82~83.5、厚9~10厘米。榻板长方形,长238、宽107、厚16米。榻面较粗糙,未经打磨。榻板周边正面及两侧均有线刻图案。榻腿共有5个。正面3个,均圆雕成狮子形;背面2个,呈靴形。

围屏线刻共有10幅画面,其中东西两侧各2幅,北面6幅。画面局部有贴金装饰,两侧及上部饰贴金柿蒂纹。线刻内容主要是反映墓主人车马出行、会见宾客等现实生活的场景。值得注意的是,北侧自西向东第四至六幅出现了胡人形象。第四幅左侧有峰峦,山

石榻的狮子榻腿
Lion-shaped leg of the stone bed

康业墓围屏石榻
Screened stone bed in the Kang Ye tomb

围屏西端自左而右第一幅线刻人物图案(局部)
The first left engraving of human figure in the western part of the screen (detail)

围屏正面自左而右第三幅线刻人物图案
The third left engraving of human figure in the middle of the screen

围屏正面自左而右第四幅线刻人物图案
The fourth left engraving of human figure in the middle of the screen

围屏正面自左而右第五幅线刻人物图案
The fifth left engraving of human figures in the middle of the screen

围屏正面自左而右第六幅线刻人物图案
The sixth left engraving of human figure in the middle of the screen

峦之下停一牛车，车旁一健牛正在卧地吃草。车的右侧跪坐2个胡人，身着胡服。一人左手举酒杯，右手执酒壶，作献酒状；另一人神态端庄，跪坐于地。第五幅上部为垂柳，中部刻一歇山顶的房子，房内坐一人，作进食状。房子左侧有2个胡人，拱手侍立。右侧也有2个胡人，或捧果盘，或持长颈瓶，身体隐于框外。下部有4个胡人，作长跪状，或捧果盘，或持长颈瓶，或执酒杯。人物形象均为身着胡服，短发，深目高鼻。第六幅上部右侧有一棵大树，树下栖息2只飞鸟。中央为一组人物出行图。左侧站4人，右侧2马，一高鼻秃头的胡人立于马匹中间。

墓志青石质，由志盖和志石组成。志盖方形，盝顶，边长45.5、厚8.5厘米。志石方形，边长46.5、厚13厘米。志文魏体，共计397字，详细介绍了墓主人的生平、族属等。从墓志志文可知，该墓墓主人名业，字元基，是康居国王的后裔，历任大天主、罗州使君、车骑大将军、雍州呼乐等职。死于大周天和六年，死后被诏增为甘州刺史。他有三子，长子汲休延，次子槃陁，次子货土。

目前国内发现的其他6座粟特人墓葬，出土的围屏石榻或石椁均为浅浮雕的艺术形式，而康业墓出土的围屏石榻则是用线刻来表现墓主人的生活场景。画面布局独特，与以往发现的有较大差异。画面的景深分为三至四个层次，顶部刻流云、飞鸟，以示远在天际；之下刻山峦、林木以示近景；人物均在高大的树荫之下，下部的坡、石、水、草为最近景。自上而下，由远及近，层次井然。在整幅画面中，各部分所占比例不同。人物背后的林木、山峦最大，约占二分之一；次为人物活动的空间，约占四分之一；之下的坡、石、水、草占四分之一。从各部分所占比例我们可以看出，作画者

围屏东端自左而右第二幅线刻人物图案
The second left engraving of human figures
in the eastern part of the screen

尽管非常重视画面中的人物活动，却用了较大的空间来表现人物活动的背景。

魏晋南北朝是我国山水画的萌芽时期，尽管有关山水画的著述不少，但独立的山水画作较少见到。该墓围屏上的线刻画作虽然不是山水画，但它在构图上对人物活动的背景给予充分的表现，是山水画萌芽及发展过程中的重要一环。总之，该墓的发现为研究北朝时期的社会生活、丧葬习俗、绘画艺术提供了珍贵的资料。

围屏西端自左而右第一幅和第二幅线刻人物图案
The first and second left engravings of human figures in the western part of the screen

6 April 2004, a Sogdian's tomb of the Northern Zhou period in the northern suburb of Xi'an City was discovered in a course of capital construction. Then it was excavated by the Xi'an Municipal Institute of Ancient Monument Preservation and Archaeology. Among the objects it yielded is a screened intact stone bed with engravings exquisite in craftsmanship and rich in content.

The tomb is located about 150 m to the north of the Northern Zhou An Jia tomb and 2,000 m or so to the west of the Northern Zhou Shi's tomb grave. It is a vaulted cave with an azimuth of 179°, and consists of a ramping passage, a corridor and a chamber. The passage is on the southern side of the chamber and has been damaged. The corridor has a roughly trapezoid plan and measures 2.16 m in length and 1.42—1.5 m in width. The chamber has a sub-quadrate plan, each side measuring 3.3 — 3.4 m. Its vault has also been damaged and thus the tomb is unknown in height. There are two covered tome-gates: the first is at the corridor entrance and is made of bricks; the second is structured of stone in the corridor.

The stone bed stands in the middle of the northern side of the chamber with the longer sites pointing to the east and west, and consists of a screen, a body and legs. The screen is made of four rectangular stone slabs. The side stones are 93.5 cm long, 82 cm high and 7 — 8.5 cm thick; the middle two, 106—111, 82—83.5 and 9—10 cm respectively. The inner walls are polished and bear ten engravings: four on the sides and six in the middle. Some details are decorated in gold foil, and the two sides and the upper zone are bordered with gold-foil four-lobed medallions.

The bed body is a rectangular stone slab, 2.38 m long, 1.07 m wide and 0.16 m thick; its surface is coarse, unpolished, and the eastern, western and southern sides are engraved with designs. It is supported with five legs: three lion-shaped in the front and two boot-shaped at the back. On the bed is an intact human skeleton in an extended supine position, head pointing to the west. Traces of silk in a few layers remain on the corpse.

Between the bed and the epitaph at the center of the chamber is a layer of plant ash, which must have been concerned with the burial custom. In the corridor and on the chamber walls, excavators found murals painted directly on the lime-plastered surface. Covered by silt and poor in condition, they call for further study as to their contents.

This is the seventh example of the Sogdians' burials with stone beds or sarcophagi discovered so far in China. The epitaphs unearthed from these tombs record in detail the tomb-owners' nationality, official career and date of entombment. The tomb-owner of the present grave, as known from his epitaph, was named Ye and also Yuanji and descended from the king of Sogdiana. He held successively the posts of Wei Da Tianzhu 魏大天

主, Luozhou Shijun 罗州使君, Ju Ji Dajiangjun 车骑大将军 and Yongzhou Hule 雍州呼乐, died in the sixth year of Tianhe reign, Northern Zhou period, and was posthumously titled Ganzhou Cishi 甘州刺史. He had three sons, who were named, from the elder to the younger, Fan Xiu Yan, Pan Tuo and Huo Zhu respectively.

The screen of the stone bed in the present tomb is the only engraved example so far discovered for its counterparts from the other six Sogdian burials are all carved in low relief. The tomb-owner's living scenes represented on it are quite different from the previously unearthed in composition and layout. The forests and mountains in the background of human figures occupy the greatest proportion of the whole carving, accounting for about a half of the total area; next comes the space for depicting people's activities, approximately one fourth; and then the hillsides, rocks, waters and grasses, also one fourth. From the engravings on the screen the Wei, Jin and Southern and Northern Dynasties period can be conjured up as the embryonic stage of Chinese landscape painting. In short, the excavation of the tomb furnishes valuable material to researching into the living and burial customs of the Sogdians that inhabited in China in the Northern Dynasties period, as well as Sino-Western cultural exchanges and ancient Chinese painting art.

石榻正面线刻凤纹图案
Phoenix engraved in the front of the bed

围屏正面自左而右第四幅至第六幅线刻人物图案
The fourth-sixth left engravings of human figures in the middle of the screen

西安唐太液池
皇家园林遗址

THE IMPERIAL GARDEN SITE
AT THE TANG TAIYECHI POOL IN XI'AN

位于唐长安城大明宫中北部的太液池以及周岸上的建筑，是唐代园林建筑的代表作，曾被唐朝大多数皇帝所使用。其始建年代可能是贞观八

太液池北岸遗址雪中工作场景
Site of exploration in the snow on the
northern shore of the Taiyechi Pool

年（634年），唐末被废弃。

2001年8月，中国社会科学院考古研究所与日本独立行政法人文化财研究所奈良文化财研究所合作，对太液池皇家园林遗址进行发掘。截止到2004年底，中日联合考古队已进行了五次发掘，发掘面积达1.6万平方米，获得了丰富的考古资料。

太液池又名蓬莱池，位于今陕西省西安市未央区大明宫乡，在龙首原的北侧。池址分为东西两部分。东池较小，略呈圆形，面积约3.3万平方米；西池较大，呈椭圆形，面积约14万平方米。发掘表明，太液池的东南池岸是夯打的驳岸，北岸中西段则为生土缓坡岸；西岸北半段也是夯土岸，但岸边为缓坡。在岸边均发现道路痕迹（车辙和路土面），与

太液池遗址干栏式建筑基础
遗存鸟瞰(上北下南)
A bird-eye's view of
the foundations of pile-
buildings on the site of
Taiyechi Pool (photo
from south to north)

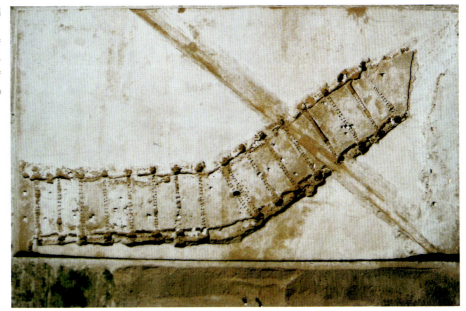

太液池遗址干栏式建筑基础
遗存(自西向东摄)
Foundations of pile-
buildings on the site of
Taiyechi Pool (photo
from west to east)

池岸的走向一致,最宽处可达25米。

在池的西岸和南岸,分别清理出廊房建筑遗迹2座和大型廊院建筑基址1处。其中西岸的F4是单面空廊建筑,西边敞开,东边用夯土墙封闭,走向与池西岸平行。残长61米,间长4.05、宽3.7米。F5位于F4南侧,为双面空廊,保存状况较差。大型廊院基址位于南岸高地,其性质是前朝殿址与太液池址之间的连接通道和过渡区。共清理出南北向和东西向的廊道各4条、南北向和东西向的独立夯土墙各1道,以及由它们间隔出的6个院落。院落

均呈长方形,大小不等,面积30~70多平方米。值得注意的是,在廊道填土中和白灰墙皮上还发现了涂有绿色、红色和黄色的壁画碎块。

水边建筑遗迹发现2处。在太液池北岸附近的沟底,清理出一组干栏式建筑基础遗存,长近70、横宽13米,由16排柱洞(每排两行)组成15个建筑单元。该建筑是架在沟上面的干栏式建筑,用成排的木柱支撑,上面有搭板构建的房屋。

太液池西北角的水道为进水渠,东北角的水道为出水渠。在池址西岸和南岸的发掘中,均发现排

望仙台
排水沟
夯墙
廊
廊
廊
廊
廊
排水沟
夯墙
廊
廊
廊
廊
排水沟
井
8口井
井
井
石料
井

太液池遗址南岸廊院建筑遗存(自北向南摄)
Remains of the corridor-and-court complex on the southern
shore of the Taiyechi Pool (photo from north to south)

水沟和水井。这表明，太液池周岸曾规划了给排水设施。大排水沟较宽且深，沟中两壁多用砖垒砌。小排水沟均与大排水沟连接，或用砖砌，或用筒瓦铺接，或用石刻水槽、陶水管相连。水井多为圆形，直径1米余，深达7～10米，有些井有砖砌的井圈。

在池址北岸的南侧池内，发现一座生土岛屿，平面略呈长方形，南北长70、东西宽50余米，上面没有建筑。该岛加上早已明确的主岛蓬莱岛，使得唐诗中提到的"三岛"有两个得到了落实。

人造园林景观遗迹共发现2处，分别位于池址东南岸和蓬莱岛南岸。在蓬莱岛南岸清理出夯土路、砖砌的小水池、池边叠石、亭基石础、平桥、假山等。这表明，蓬莱岛是太液池中的一座园林式岛屿。《旧唐书》等文献也多次记载，唐穆宗、文宗、宣宗等常邀文臣近士到此岛游玩。

遗址内出土大量遗物，有砖瓦、石构件、陶瓷器、铜铁器、骨器、玻璃串珠、贝雕、封泥、螺蚌壳等。建筑材料数量最多，有条形墙砖、方形莲花纹地砖、四叶纹方砖、瑞兽葡萄纹方砖、素面方砖、板瓦、筒瓦、莲花瓦当、鸱尾等。许多是经过渗炭处理、表面光滑黑亮的砖瓦，少数为琉璃瓦。有些砖瓦上还模印有工匠姓氏、年月、窑名、吉祥语等。

石雕包括柱础石、雕像、石插座等。在南岸一小院内出土一件残石象，象背披有莲花纹鞍，上置莲花宝座，雕刻精美。

陶瓷器以白瓷为主，也有黑瓷、青瓷、三彩和红陶、灰陶器，器类有碗、盘、枕、盒、注壶、唾壶、背水壶、瓶等。其中许多是来自各地的御用贡品，如碗底带有"官"字和"盈"字款的白瓷碗、仿金银的白瓷葵口碗。铜钱有"开元通宝"和"乾元重宝"。

唐太液池皇家园林遗址的发掘，极大地弥补了古代文献记载的不足，为研究中国古代园林建筑提供了第一手资料。

The Taiyechi Pool and the buildings on its shore, which lie in the middle and north of the Daminggong Palace, Tang Chang'an City, constituted the most important imperial garden and were used by most of the Tang emperors. As a representative work of Tang gardening, it was probably built in the 8th year of Zhenguan reign (AD 634) and abandoned in the late Tang. Its site is located at Daminggong Township of Weiyang District in present-day Xi'an, on the northern side of Mt. Longshouyuan. The pool-site consists of two parts: The eastern part is smaller in area, has a roughly circular plan, and occupies an area of 33,000 sq m; the western one is larger, oval in plan, and about 140,000 sq m in area.

In the spring of 2003 and that of 2004, the Collaborative Archaeological Team, Institute of Archaeology, CASS, and Japan Nara Cultural Properties Research Institute carried out here archaeological excavations. They made important discoveries successively on the northern shore of Taiyechi Pool, the southern edge of Penglaidao Island and the southern shore of Taiyechi Pool.

Between the northern shore of Taiyechi and the island on the pool's southern side, on the bottom of a gully, they revealed the foundations of pile-buildings. The whole complex looks roughly like the letter "V" in plan with a bend of 135°, and measures nearly 70 m in length and about 13 m in width. On the foundations, 16 parallel rows of column holes form 15 building spaces, and stone structural members (railing stones, bearing stones and plinths) as well as building materials (decorated bricks, square bricks, lotus-flower design tile-ends and ridge ornaments) are scattered in debris.

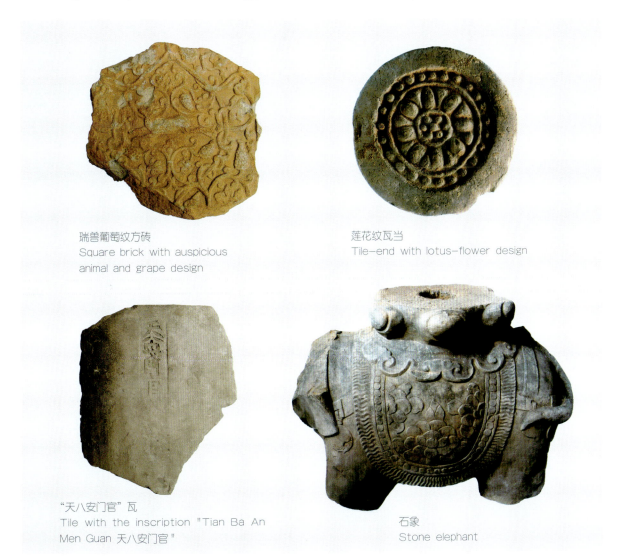

瑞兽葡萄纹方砖
Square brick with auspicious animal and grape design

莲花纹瓦当
Tile-end with lotus-flower design

"天八安门官" 瓦
Tile with the inscription "Tian Ba An Men Guan 天八安门官"

石象
Stone elephant

135

These suggest that the original buildings were structured on piles (stilts), which were erected in the gully and supported timber floors and entire superstructures.

At the southern edge of Penglaidao Island, excavation uncovered plenty of remains of garden sights, including rammed-earth paths, brick pools, man-made rockeries, pebble-paved troughs and channels, and pavilion foundations. It can be concluded that Penglaidao was a garden-style island with a charming view.

On the southern shore of Taiyechi Pool, exploration brought to light a ruined large corridor-and-court complex. It is located on the north-to-south central axis with the Hanyuandian, Xuanzhengdian and Zichengdian pavilions on the south, the Taiyechi Pool on the north, the Penglaidian and Lingqidian pavilions on the east, and the Hall of Golden Chimes on the west. It must have been the passageway between the frontal imperial court and the rear garden area. The ruins consist of rammed-earth walls, corridor vestiges and courtyard remains. The wall surface is made smooth and coated with red or white lime mortar, and bears traces of paintings in some zones. The corridor floor is left over in certain thickness and flanked by brick aprons. In addition, six wells and three covered drains were discovered in the courtyard.

Numbers of treasures were unearthed in the two seasons of excavation. The structural members of palaces include wall and floor bricks, flat and cylindrical tiles, lotus-flower design tile-ends, ridge ornaments and stone plinths and lamp-stands. A lot of bricks and tiles are inscribed with the names of governmental kilns and masters, as well as auspicious words. Among the porcelain utensils used in palaces are bowls, dishes, pillows, boxes and pots. They belong largely to white ware and partly to black and celadon wares; and three-color glazed and marbled ware products occur in some cases. A few porcelain shards with the characters "Guan 官" or "Ying 盈" are especially valuable.

仿金银器的白瓷碗
White porcelain bowl in imitation of gold-and-silver ware

带 "官" 字款的白瓷碗底
Bases of white porcelain bowls with the inscription "Guan 官"

带 "盈" 字款的白瓷碗底
Base of a white porcelain bowl with the inscription "Ying 盈"

白瓷睡盂
White porcelain spittoon

西藏阿里噶尔县
"琼隆银城" 遗址

KHYUNG-LUNG DNGUL-MKHAR SITE
IN GAR COUNTY OF NGARI, TIBET

2004年6~7月,四川大学历史文化学院考古系、四川大学中国藏学研究所"边疆考古课题组"与西藏自治区文物局联合,对阿里地区象泉河上游地区进行了较为全面的田野调查,在噶尔县门士乡境内调查发现多处古代遗存,其中尤以象雄时代的"琼隆银城"遗址引人注目。

"琼隆银城"遗址地处西藏西部的札达盆地东缘,东北距门士乡驻地约12公里,地貌为河谷湿地与平顶山丘相间。遗址位于一座较平的山丘顶部,地势北高南低,分为A、B、C、D四个区,总面积约13万平方米。

A区位于遗址南部,面积约6万平方米。调查发现多处地面建筑遗迹,由砾岩岩块或大砾石砌建,分为90余个建筑单元,包括防御性建筑、生活居住建筑、公共性建筑(宗教祭祀类)、生活附属设施建筑等。防御建筑遗迹分布在山顶,居高凭险,由多重防墙和与之连接的方形堡垒、暗道构成。居住遗迹的平面一般是方形或圆形,为多间式或单间式。公共建筑遗迹包括前有石砌阶梯的较大建筑,和可能是祭台的长条形石台。生活附属设施主要有两类,一类是附属于居址的牲圈,另一类是居址群之间的圆形大坑,其用途可能是人畜用水的蓄水坑。A区可能是生活区。

B区位于遗址北部西缘,面积近1.5万平方米。建筑遗迹共有13个单元,主要是建在山顶崖边的防墙、堡垒等防御工事,另发现与宗教仪式活动相关的建筑遗迹,和一个地道入(出)口。防墙遗迹用砾岩岩块和少量砾石、石板砌成,现存长度近300米,沿山顶崖边而建,包括主墙和护墙两部分。主墙现存宽0.6~0.8米,高仅0.1~0.3米。

C区位于遗址北部东缘,与B区之间有一低洼的沟谷相隔,面积近1万平方米。共发现建筑遗迹20个单元,主要是防墙、堡垒,其平面布局是一个L形建筑群。堡垒平面略呈方形,南北两端辟有出入口,四面墙体由低到高逐层收分,呈高台状。

D区位于略低于前三区的另一座山丘顶上。调查发现遗迹8处,全部为防御工事建筑。从整体布局上看,D区可能是扼守遗址北端的防守营地。

文化遗物主要是遗址地面的采集品,少数为清理遗迹所获,可分为石器、陶器、金属器、骨蚌器、动物骨块等。其中石器数量最多,种类有片状砺石或石磨盘、石臼、打制砍斫器等。部分石器上有红色颜料的痕迹。陶器皆为残片,陶系多见夹砂红褐陶。可辨器形的仅有罐类,少数饰有绳纹。金属器包括铁质甲片、铜饰残片等。骨蚌器多为装饰品,另有部分骨料以及骨质工具残件。遗址内出土一尊双面青铜神像,其头部分前后两面,面容狰狞,具有印度早期造像的特征。该像可能与西藏西部的原始本教有关。

据史籍记载,象雄(汉文史书亦有"羊同"、"女国"之称)曾在吐蕃王朝建立之前在今阿里一带立国。它雄踞藏西北,以本教为国教,并有自己独特的文字系统,曾先后建立过不同的都城与城堡,并设大臣分掌国事。公元7世纪,吐蕃赞普松赞干布灭了象雄。

据当地本教经典记载,"琼隆银城"曾是象雄王子次巴朗卡时期的王都,或称"琼隆卡尔孜",即"山顶鹏城"之意。"银城"的由来据说与城堡所处

"琼隆银城" 遗址远眺（自南向北摄）
A distant view of the Khyung–lung Dngul–mkhar site (photo from south to north)

A区建筑遗迹群(自北向南摄)
Vestiges of buildings in Area A (photo from north to south)

A区居住遗迹
Vestiges of dwellings
in Area A

A 区蓄水坑遗迹
Remains of water-storing hollow

B 区北端的护坡遗迹
Vestiges of slope-protecting structures at the northern end of Area B

的灰白色砾岩山顶有关。

对采集陶器、石器等的分析表明，"琼隆银城"遗址与其下游的皮央·东嘎、格布赛鲁等遗址或墓群中的早期遗存相似，其年代可能与之相当，即稍早于吐蕃王朝时期。而遗址出土木质样品的¹⁴C 数据表明，其年代可能在公元 5～7 世纪之间。

此外，在该遗址附近数公里半径内还发现古墓群、石器地点、立石遗迹、建筑遗址等。如位于"琼隆银城"西北 3 公里处的泽蚌遗址，占地面积达 50 万平方米，是一处集地面石构建筑、墓葬群、生产设施为一体的大型遗址。该遗址中的 M2 是一座大型积石墓，用砾石垒砌的墓丘平面呈长方形，长 62、宽 17.3 米。逐层向上收分，略呈覆斗形，残高 3～6 米。墓丘背面有石砌踏道，以及可能是祭坛的圆形石台。从积石墓丘的形制来看，墓主应有极高的地位，并且可能与象雄王国有着密切关联。

C区西缘的防墙遗迹
Vestiges of parapets at the western edge of Area C

C区出土的动物骨骸
Faunal remains from Area C

In June to July 2004, the Archaeology Department of History and Culture college and the Border-land Archaeology Project Group of the Institute of Chinese Tibetology, Sichuan University, and the Bureau of Culture, Tibet Autonomous Region, organized jointly the Archaeological Team for the survey of the Xiangquan River Valley. They carried out an extensive field investigation in the upper Xiangquan River valley, Ngari Prefecture, in June to July, and discovered in Menshi Township of Gar County a lot of ancient remains maybe belonging to the "Zhang Zhung" period

in Tibet. The most attractive is the Khyung-lung dngul-mkhar site left over from that time.

This site is situated at the eastern edge of the Zanda Depression in western Tibct, about 12 km southwest to the seat of Menshi Township. Lying on the relatively level summit of a hill, it has a terrain higher in the north and lower in the south, with an elevation of 4,300 m. It occupies an area of about 130,000 sq m, and can be divided into Areas A, B, C, and D.

Area A is in the south of the site. Surveys discovered here a lot of remains of surface buildings made of

在遗址采集的石磨盘
Stone quern from the site

在遗址采集的石臼
Stone mortars from the site

在遗址采集的砍砸器
Chopping tools from the site

青铜神像
God statuette in bronze

blocks of conglomerate or boulders. Among them are defensive buildings (parapets and fortifications), dwelling houses, common buildings (religious and sacrificial) and auxiliary living structures. The terrain is relatively gentle, the vestiges are densely distributed, the buildings vary in form and use. So there must have been the resident quarter of the site.

Area B lies at the western edge of the north of the site. It is higher than Area

考古工作人员在遗址现场做记录
Archaeological workers taking records on the site

A in terrain. It measures about 350 m in length from the west to the east and 15—50 m in width from the north to the south, occupying an area of nearly 15,000 sq m. Exploration revealed 13 units of building vestiges (mainly remaining parapets and fortifications), as well as ruins probably related to religious activities. The parapets are nearly 300 m in total remaining length. They are built along the edge of cliffs on the summit. Their main part is on the ground of the summit and the protective part on the outer side, below cliff-slopes, both built of man-chiseled conglomerate blocks and a small quantity of boulders and stones. Besides, excavators found the entrance of a tunnel.

Area C is situated at the eastern edge of the north of the site. It is also higher than Area A, and is separated from Area B by a low-lying ravine. Measuring nearly 300 m in length from the west to the east and about 30 m in width from the north to the south, it occupyies an area approximately of 10,000 sq m. The main building vestiges discovered are also remains of parapets and fortifications, totaling 20 units.

Area D is located at the northern end of the site. The vestiges are distributed on the summit of another hill that is a little lower than the above-described areas. Only eight plots of remains are recorded through survey, and all of them are fortifications. Area D

might have been a campsite to guard the northern end of the site.

The cultural relics discovered fall into stone implements, pottery, metals, bone and shell objects and animal bones. The stone implements vary in size and belong to the grinding flake, quern and mortar with traces of red pigment in some cases, and chipped tool. The pottery vessels are all broken, the typologically discernible belong to the jar, and some shards bear cord marks. A noteworthy find is a god statuette in bronze. Peculiar in appearance, it has double robust faces in the front and at the back respectively. The looks and carriage are distinctly different from those of Buddhist images in Tibet. This sculpture might have been concerned with proto-Bon in western Tibet.

According to records in Tibetan and Chinese historical documents, the Zhang Zhung people founded their state in the Ngari area before the founding of the Tubo Dynasty. They were converted to Bon as their national religion and created their own distinctive writing system. Their state existed until the Tubo btsan-po Songtsan Gambo conquered it in the 7th century. The available pottery objects, stone implements and ^{14}C-dating data indicate that the site can be assigned to the time between the 5th and the 7th century, a little earlier than the Tubo Dynasty period.

江西玉山
渎口窑

DUKOU KILN-SITE IN YUSHAN, JIANGXI

渎口窑位于玉山县下镇渎口村东面约1公里的小山坡上，由邻近的3个窑包组成，下镇溪和八都溪从窑址的南部蜿蜒流过。该窑址主要烧造青瓷器。2004年5~7月，在玉山县博物馆的配合下，江西省文物考古研究所对其中的一个窑包进行了抢救性发掘。该窑包地势北高南低，东西长约100、南北宽约60米，面积约6000平方米。瓷片堆积厚度最深处达5米余。我们开5×5米探方42个，发掘面积1050平方米。

遗址北部地势较高，为窑炉所在地；南部地势较平坦，为作坊区。我们在北部揭露出窑炉3座，南北向，顺南坡平行排列。其中一座较完整，为斜坡式龙窑，在山坡上挖斜底隧道形成窑室，利用原山体作为窑壁。龙窑总长16.5米，分为窑床、火膛、焚口三部分。窑床呈长条形，长10.4、宽1.8米，坡度15°，窑顶不存。窑壁用黏土敷就，残高0.2米，厚约18厘米。窑室底部是平坦的斜坡，经火烧已呈深红色。火膛近圆形，直径3.9米。顶部已毁，残高0.7米。火膛壁用石块垒砌，面向火膛的一面较平坦，且有一定的弧度。火膛底部用两块

渎口窑窑址全景(自南向北摄)
A panoramic view of the Dukou kiln-site
(photo from south to north)

窑址近景(自西向东摄)
A close view of the kiln-site (photo from west to east)

龙窑出土现状(自南向北摄)
A dragon kiln in excavation (photo from south to north)

大石间隔,分成两部分。近窑床的火膛北端较高,用小石粒铺就,中部有一条V形火道。焚口平面形状呈梯形,壁用大石块堆砌,长2.44、宽1.85～2.23米。

北部的废瓷片堆积以窑炉为中心,大体可分为两部分。其中西坡堆积较薄,平均厚度约1.5米,器物绝大部分是壶类器。东坡堆积较厚,最厚处5米余,器物主要是碗碟盏类。

在较平坦的窑包南部,发现一座建筑,已残。大致坐西朝东,有前后两室。墙基用石块铺成,墙

体为泥坯。前室中部有一长方形天井,长2.5、宽2米。井壁用石块垒成,深约0.25米。为使天井排水通畅,在其西面采用双排水系统,用陶制排水管相套而成。

该窑址是一处烧造青瓷器的民间中型窑场,以烧造日常生活用品为主。此次发掘共出土完整和可复原的器物2000余件,可分为生活用具、瓷塑、建筑构件、窑具等。生活用具主要有盘口壶、直口壶、喇叭口壶、碗、盏、罐、盆、杯、钵、器盖、网坠、扑满、瓶、熏炉、粉盒,以及辗磨茶叶的工具——

辗轮，其中壶的数量和种类最多。窑具有支烧垫墩、轮轴帽、垫饼和荡箍。支烧垫墩中空，高15～20厘米。轮轴帽近圆柱状，平顶，下部有一圆形孔。支钉一般呈长条形，垫饼则利用废弃的碗底做成。

瓷胎分为白色和灰褐色两种，以灰褐色居多。釉色主要是青釉和酱褐色釉，另外有极少量的黑釉。青瓷占绝大多数，釉色青中泛黄，流釉显著，极少开片。在施釉方面一般采用荡釉和浸釉，釉不及底。以素面为多，只有碗装饰有划花或刻花的莲瓣、蕉叶和水波纹。部分器物饰釉下褐釉点彩。

渎口窑的器物均为裸烧，不见匣钵。为避免生烧现象，抬升器物在窑内的高度，当时人用支烧垫墩来支撑器物。相同规格的碗叠烧时，采用支钉间隔。大碗套小碗或盏时，用垫饼加以间隔。碗盏类因个体较小，一般采用叠烧。由于器物较重，叠烧的往往容易变形，废品较多。

渎口窑以烧造青瓷为主，胎多灰白，质粗而坚，釉色青中闪黄，流釉明显，开片少，装饰技法主要是划花或刻花，花样简单，主要是花卉，这些都具有越窑的典型特征。因此，渎口窑应属越窑系统。从该窑出土的壶来看，其始烧年代大致为晚唐。窑址出土"元丰通宝"铜钱，器物未见芒口器，并出土影青斗笠碗和龙泉炉残片。由此推断，其终烧时间约当在北宋中晚期。

瓶
Vase

扑满
Coin bank

盘口壶
Dish-shape-mouthed pot

短颈壶
Short-necked pot

长颈双系壶
Double-looped long-necked pot

The Dukou kiln-site is situated at Dukou Village in Xiazhen Town about 11 km east of the seat of Yushan County, on hill-slopes approximately 1 km east of the village. It consists of the remains of three celadon-firing kilns. In May to July 2004, the Jiangxi Provincial Institute of Cultural Relics and Archaeology carried out a rescuing excavation to explore one of the kilns.

The excavated kiln remains are about 100 m long from the west to the east and 60 m wide from the north to the south, and form a terrain higher in the north and lower in the south. The porcelain shard deposits are five meters thick at the greatest depth. The kiln itself is in the north and consists of three furnaces, which are in the sloping style and belong to the type of dragon kiln. One of the furnaces left over only the baking chamber; another, a part of kiln bed. The roughly intact one is also damaged at the top. It consists of a kiln bed, a baking chamber and a firing chamber (close to the mouth) and measures 16.5 m in total length. The workshop area is in the relatively level south. There is a building with a courtyard at the center. It faces to the east and consists of two rooms arranged one behind another. The rear room has been destroyed. The central courtyard has a rectangular plan. On the western and southern sides are pottery drainpipes leading to the outside.

The Dukou kilns yielded mainly celadon, and also a small amount of black and brown wares. The products

彩绘鱼塑
Painted porcelain fish

粉盒
Toilet box

支烧垫墩
Fire clay pillar

are generally grayish-white in body, and coarse and hard in texture. The glaze is yellowish-green with distinct traces of floating and, occasionally, cracking. The decorative techniques are principally incising and carving simple motifs, especially floral designs. Among the kiln

implements are fire clay pillars, bowls of wheel axles, fire clay discs and wheel tires. The unearthed intact or restorable objects number more than 2,000 pieces. They belong mostly to daily utensils and fall into the types of pot (greatest in number and variety, including those with dish-shaped, straight or flared mouth), bowl, *yu* vase, jar, basin, cup, lid, net-weight, coin bank, incense burner, toilet box, and grinding wheel. In addition, there are porcelain sculptures and structural members in a small number. All products are fired without saggers.

The Dukou kilns were located in the east of present-day Jiangxi and formed a medium-scale civilian factory producing celadon. They functioned for a short period of time from the late Tang to the middle and late Northern Song and belonged to the Yue Yao system. The excavation of the site provided important material data for researching into the history of ceramics in the Jiangxi region and the exchange between the porcelain production of Zhejiang and that of Jiangxi in ancient times.

江苏扬州
宋大城北门水门遗址

WATER VALVE SITE AT THE NORTHERN GATE
OF THE GREAT SONG IN YANGZHOU, JIANGSU

宋大城水门遗址位于扬州市玉带河与漕河交汇口的东南隅，其东部是宋大城北门遗址。2003年春季该遗址被发现后，中国社会科学院考古研究所与南京博物院、扬州市文物局联合，于2003年11月～2004年5月先后3次对遗址进行试掘和发掘。在南北长约21、东西宽约12.5米的范围内，揭露出水门北段的东西石壁、东壁滑槽、门道以及河床内的木桩、木板、石板等遗迹。

主城墙位于水门石壁的东西两侧。其中东侧的主城墙墙壁保存较好，城墙顶部距水门底部残高约5米。该城墙从五代一直沿用到元代。

水门的主体部分由东西两侧石壁构成，石壁外侧为主城墙，北端与北段水门摆手连接。已发掘部

宋大城北门水门遗址西部清理现场图(自南向北摄)
Site of excavation in the west of the water valve
site of the northern city-gate, Great Song Yangzhou
City (photo from south to north)

宋大城北门水门遗址全景(自南向北摄)
A full view of the water valve site of the northern city-gate,
Great Song Yangzhou City (photo from south to north)

宋大城北门水门东壁的砌石和滑槽(自西向东摄)
Stone courses and slide in the eastern wall of the water valve at the northern city-gate of Great Song Yangzhou City (photo from west to east)

分的两壁，东西石壁方位角均为5°，南北方向长16米，与主城墙垂直。两侧石壁各宽约2.4米，两壁内边之间相距7.1米。东壁保存最高处有20层，高达3.6米，石壁之上残存零散的砌砖，应该属于石壁上层砌砖被破坏后的残留。西侧石壁因河道变化及后世破坏，仅残存底层砌石。两侧石壁内边之间即为水门的门洞。在底层石条之下，铺有夹杂大量碎瓦砾的青灰色衬底。

东侧石壁靠近最高处，有一条竖向的滑槽。滑槽用"L"或"Π"字形的两类石条拼合而成，平面呈方形，边长0.26、高约3.4米。滑槽底部开口于底层石条之上，内底部西北角有残砖1块。

门道方位角与水门石壁相同，与主城墙垂直。门道内是水门中间河床之上的堆积，主要是元、明时代的堆积。水门券顶范围不清楚，目前残存的可能是门洞券顶倒塌砖的堆积。此处倒塌砖的规格较多，砖之间勾缝使用了大量的白灰膏。

"摆手"一词源自《营造法式》的记载，指水门东西两壁出门道后呈"八"字形的部分。水门北段摆手的做法与水门门道处的石壁相同，均由石条垒砌而成。西侧摆手残存6层砌石，高约1.06、南北长约6.5米；东侧摆手残存12层砌石，高2.1、长11米。

水门东侧砌石底部以下，共清理出基础木桩13根，直径多在15～20厘米之间。木桩顶部平整，大致在同一水平面上。木桩之上铺有一层夹杂碎瓦砾的青灰色填垫层，厚约20厘米。这层填垫层取平之后，再在其上垒砌水门的石壁。

东西石壁之间有南北向排列整齐的木桩，这些木桩可以分为3种类型，即护岸木桩、"地钉"和为防止船只进出水门之际碰撞石壁而设置的高木桩。在第3列和第4列木桩之间，还发现埋有厚约10厘米的木板。这些木板应该也是用来固定地钉的。在上述木桩之间嵌有若干石板，石板可能是《营造法式》中所记载的"掰石"。

此外，在凤凰桥下的玉带河东驳岸下发现了宋代驳岸，我们对之进行了局部发掘。驳岸方位角为351°，与水门北段西侧摆手相同。驳岸倾斜角为向西偏约20°，残存砌砖11层。

遗物主要出土于河道沉积堆积中，有唐至明代的瓷器、铜镜、鎏金铜器、铜钱、铁器、铭文砖、玻璃器残件等。出土遗物中种类最丰富的是元代瓷

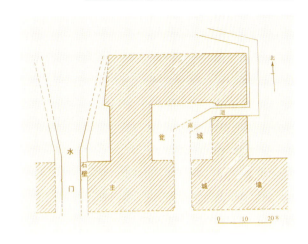

扬州宋大城北门水门遗址位置示意图
Schematic map of the location of the water valve site at the northern city-gate of Great Song Yangzhou City

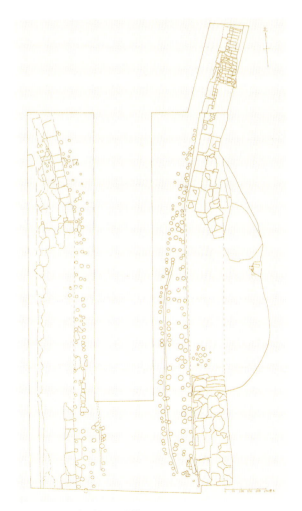

宋大城北门水门遗址平面图
Plan of the water valve site at the northern city-gate of Great Song Yangzhou City

元龙泉窑圈底杯
Round-bottomed cups of Longquan ware, Yuan period

元龙泉窑龙纹碗底
Base of a dragon design bowl of Longquan ware, Yuan period

器，出土量最大的是铜钱和铁钱。还出土了四犬纹铜镜、柳毅传书人物故事纹铜镜、"寿"字镜、海兽葡萄镜、"元宝"铸铁范以及与行船有关的铁链、镐头等。

　　宋大城北门水门遗址的发现，证明了文献中关于宋大城有水门的记载。水门是为了解决城墙跨河问题而修建的门道设施，既可以通水行船，又可以加强河道防御。宋大城北门水门的始建年代不早于五代，废弃于元代，门洞券顶可能倒塌于明代。目前揭露出来的水门遗址，可能是南宋时期的遗存。

明红绿彩樽式炉
Red-and-green-painted *zun* three-leg vase shape incense burner, Ming period

元青花"寿"字高足杯
Blue-and-white goblet with the character "Shou 寿," Yuan period

元青花龙纹高足杯
Blue-and-white goblet with dragon design, Yuan period

宋代柳毅传书人物故事纹铜镜
Bronze mirror with a scene of the variety
play *Liu Yi Chuan Shu* (《柳毅传书》), Song period

四犬镜
Four-dog design mirror

In March to May 2004, the Jiangsu Tang Yangzhou City Archaeological Team (jointly organized by the Institute of Archaeology, CASS, the Nanjing Museum and the Yangzhou Municipal Bureau of Cultural Relics) carried out a rescuing excavation on the water valve site at the confluence of the Yudai River and the Grand Canal. They revealed, in the northern section of the water valve, the eastern and western stone walls, the slide in the eastern wall, the water passageway, the bent walls and a part of the embankment-protecting stone wall, and, in the riverbed, the remaining wood stakes and planks. Based on these findings they clarified preliminarily the layout of the water valve. The unearthed numerous objects belong to the time from the Tang to the Yuan period, and fall into porcelain, iron ware, bronze mirrors, copper coins, inscribed bricks, and glass.

佛头瓷塑像
Porcelain Buddha-head

The rammed-earth city-wall recovered on the site functioned from the Five Dynasties period to the Yuan Dynasty. At the place where the river course passes through the city-wall, there remain stone walls, a slide, bank-protecting stakes, ground nails and the debris of the destroyed vault of the passageway. Outside the city-wall, bent walls and embankment protecting stone walls were found along the riverbanks. Judging from the excavated ruins, the water valve must have been built no earlier than the Five Dynasties period and abandoned in the Yuan period, and the vault of the passageway may have collapsed in the Ming period. The stratigraphic relationship of the water valve site and the ruined barbican of the northern gate of the Great Song Yangzhou City as well as the building techniques of the water valve suggest that the presently revealed water valve site must be remains of the Southern Song period.

The discovery of the site verified the literal record on the existence of water valves in the Great Song Yangzhou City and the related statement in the *Yingzao Fashi* (《营造 法式》 *Building Standards*). Well-preserved in layout and remaining intact in structure, the site reflects clearly that the water valve along with the northern gate and its barbican formed a important hub of land and water communications in the northern Yangzhou City of the Song-Yuan period. The excavation furnishes important material data to studying the land and water communications and historical aspect of Song-Yuan Yangzhou City.

河南汝州
张公巷窑址

ZHANGGONGXIANG KILN-SITE
IN RUZHOU, HENAN

张公巷窑址在汝州市区东部偏南，位于中大街与张公巷的交汇处。遗址中心区面积约3600平方米，皆被居民住房和城区道路所压。2004年2~4月，河南省文物考古研究所在张公巷的东、西两侧分别开挖探方2个，发掘面积124平方米。清理出不同时期的房基4座、井4眼、灶6个、灰坑79个和过滤池1个，出土了一批张公巷窑生产的瓷器和窑具。

这次发掘出土的遗物分为唐、宋、金元、明清四个阶段，其中唐代的遗物有白釉、黑釉、黄釉、花釉瓷和三彩器等。宋代遗物以白釉、黑釉瓷为主，器形有碗、罐、瓶、盆等。此外还出土极少量的张公巷窑生产的青釉瓷器碎片和窑具。金元时期是张公巷窑的繁荣时期，在清理的79个灰坑中，有59个属于这一时期。明清遗存有井和房基。值得一提的是，在J2内出土一批精美的青花瓷，器形有

T4④B层下遗迹
Vestiges beneath Layer 4B, Square T4

器盖
Lid

盖托
Saucer

鹅颈鼓腹瓶
Goose—neck swell—belly vase

T3 ⑥层瓷片堆积
Deposits of porcelain shards in Layer 6, Square T3

碗、盘、碟、杯等。

　　本次发掘揭露的灰坑中，有20个灰坑内出土张公巷窑生产的青釉瓷或素烧坯残片，以H88、H95和H101为代表。H88开口于T4④B层下，平面呈椭圆形，坑口长0.8、宽0.58、深0.24米。坑内堆积绝大多数是张公巷窑生产的青釉瓷，能复原的器物有44件。H95开口于T4④B层下，圆形，口径2.7、深1.1米，内填灰土，含大量草木灰。出土遗物以匣钵、垫饼和素烧器残片为主，其次是张公巷窑生产的青釉瓷。

　　H101开口于T4北部第5层下，近圆形，袋状，口径2.3、深1.4～1.9米。坑内堆积可分为4层。第1～3层含较多草木灰，出土遗物以匣钵、垫饼、支钉和素烧器残片为主，瓷器残片不多。第4层出土大量的瓷器残片，能复原的器物多达10余种、100多件，其中绝大多数是张公巷窑生产的青釉瓷。

　　此外还发现过滤池一处。开口于T4④B层下，南部被J4打破。该池残长2.2、宽1.2米。四壁用长方砖砌成，底面呈北高南低的坡状，铺一层大小不等的河卵石。池内填土分为

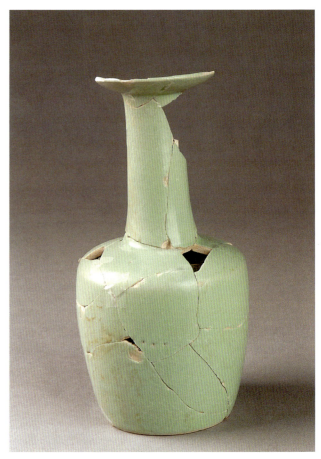

盘口细颈瓶
Dish-mouthed slender-necked vase

花口板沿平底盘
Flat-bottomed dish with lobed rim

花口折腹圈足盘
Ring-foot dish with lobed rim
and carinate belly

两层。第1层内含较多草木灰和烧土颗粒，出土遗物以匣钵、垫饼和青釉瓷、素烧坯残片为主。第2层堆积以灰白色和粉红色的块状制坯原料为主。

遗物除青釉瓷之外，白釉、黑釉、豆青釉、钧釉和白地黑花瓷等与该窑址没有直接关系。所谓的青釉瓷是张公巷烧制的唯一产品。从整体上看，它既不同于临汝窑的豆青釉，也有别于宝丰清凉寺汝窑的天青釉。釉色可分为卵青、淡青、灰青、青绿等。器物薄胎、薄釉，釉面的玻璃质感较强。胎骨有粉白、灰白、洁白和少量浅灰色，胎质细腻坚实。器形有碗、花口折腹圈足盘、花口板沿平底盘、椭圆裹足洗、椭圆平底洗、圆形平底洗、板沿平底洗、四方平底盘、盘口细颈瓶、鹅颈鼓腹瓶、盏、盏托、堆塑熏炉、套盒、器盖等。带圈足的器物以直圈足为主，碗、盘类器物的圈足上常见透明釉，露胎，部分圈足底面无釉。

这些器物往往采用垫烧，也有少量支烧的。器底支钉分三、四和五枚，支钉痕呈规整的小米粒状。窑具以匣钵、垫饼和垫圈为主。匣钵有浅腹漏斗状、深腹漏斗状、浅腹筒状和深腹筒状四种。值得注意的是，这些匣钵的外壁常常涂抹耐火泥，此工艺仅见于宝丰清凉寺汝窑。

由于发掘面积有限，地层堆积和灰坑打破关系复杂，该窑的烧造年代尚难断定。张公巷青釉瓷的造型、釉色、烧造工艺等明显承继了汝窑的风格。从地层堆积看，元代张公巷是繁荣的居民生活区，设窑烧造的可能性不大。因此我们认为，张公巷窑烧造青瓷的年代大致在北宋末至元代初年。

深腹碗
Deep-bellied bowl

深腹碗底部
Base of a deep-bellied bowl

椭圆平底洗
Flat-bottomed oval washer

椭圆平底洗底部
Base of a flat-bottomed oval washer

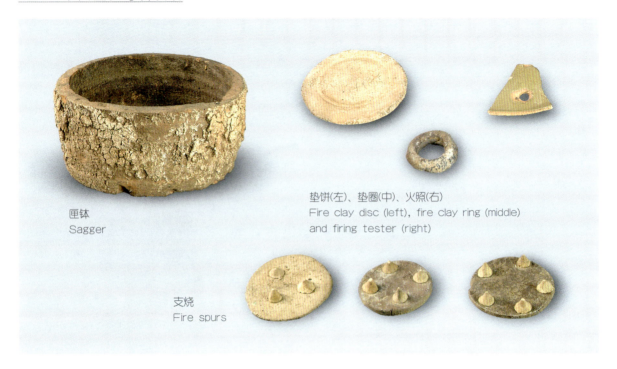

匣钵
Sagger

垫饼(左)、垫圈(中)、火照(右)
Fire clay disc (left), fire clay ring (middle)
and firing tester (right)

支烧
Fire spurs

The Zhanggongxiang kiln-site lies in the south of eastern Ruzhou City proper, with the central part occupying an area of about 3,600 sq m. In February to April 2004, the Henan Provincial Institute of Cultural Relics and Archaeology excavated it by opening two squares measuring 8 × 8 m (T3) and 5 × 13 m (T4) respectively. In the excavated area of 124 sq m, they revealed 4 house-foundations, 4 wells, 6 cooking ranges, 79 ash-pits and an elutriation pond of different periods, and brought to light a number of porcelain products and kiln implements.

The site is complex in stratigraphic deposition and rich in the variety of remaining objects. Among the finds, however, only the porcelain of green-glazed ware is produced from the Zhanggongxiang Kiln, while the rest, including the utensils of white-, black-, bean-green- and Jun-glazed and black-and-white wares, all have no direct relationship with the kiln.

On the whole, this kind of green-glazed porcelain resembles neither the bean-green-glazed ware from the Linru Kiln, nor the sky-blue-glazed products from the Ru Kiln at Baofeng Qingliangsi. Its glaze color varies from egg blue and light bluish green to darker bluish gray, blue-green and sky-clearing blue. The products feature the thin body and the strong glassiness of the thin glaze coating. The body color is powder-white,

grayish-white, pure white or light gray in some cases. The body texture is fine and solid, better than that of Ru ware. In type there are bowls, carinate-bellied ring-foot dishes, flat-bottomed washers, square dishes, larger and smaller lobed dishes, dish-mouthed vases, saucers, incense burners with designs in high relief, sets of boxes, lids, etc. On the base are traces of spurs with three to five points. The ring-foot of the bowl and dish is often coated with clear glaze, but its base has no glaze in some cases. These vessels are usually fired on spacers and occasionally on spurs.

The kiln implements are mainly saggers and spacers. The saggers fall into four types: shallow-bellied funnel-shaped, deep-bellied funnel-shaped, shallow-bellied cylindrical, and deep-bellied cylindrical. It is noteworthy that round 60% of the unearthed saggers are coated with refractory clay on the outer wall. This technical means was recorded on the Ru kiln-site at Baofeng Qingliangsi.

Judging by the unearthed objects and stratigraphic evidence, it can be preliminarily concluded that the Zhanggongxiang Kiln functioned roughly from the late Northern Song to the early Yuan period. Yielding products elaborate in workmanship and first-class in quantity, it was clearly different from usual civilian kilns and must have been a governmental workshop.

湖南宁远
玉琯岩宋代建筑遗址

SONG PERIOD BUILDING-SITE
AT YUGUANYAN IN NINGYUAN, HUNAN

玉琯岩遗址位于宁远县城东南约34公里处的山间盆地中，总面积约3.2万平方米。中心坐标北纬25°20′、东经111°59′，海拔高程368米，地属九疑山九疑洞村。遗址背依舜源峰，面向五臣峰，西望子江，北邻砯水，现地貌多为呈梯级分布的稻田耕土。

2003年12月~2004年10月，湖南省文物考古研究所对该遗址进行考古发掘，发掘面积5000平方米。遗址表层因受耕作与建设活动的破坏，南宋前期的建筑遗迹（F11~F14）仅有零星残留，但北宋时期的建筑基址保存相对完好。北宋建筑基址包含大殿、廊庑、道路、排水设施等四类遗迹。

大殿F15位于该组建筑群的北端，平面为长方形，长24.8、宽15.2米，门阔5.8米。四周用灰白胎红衣条砖砌出墙基，殿内以磉礅为柱基，殿前用方砖铺设散水。磉礅24个，4行6列，边长160~

遗址环境(自南向北摄)
Environments of the site
(photo from south to north)

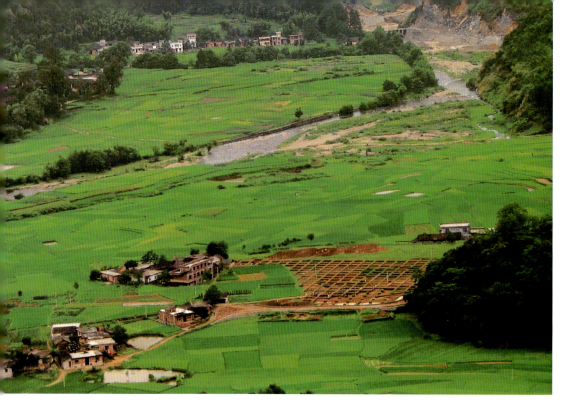

遗址发掘区全景(自东向西摄)
A full view of the excavated area of
the site (photo from east to west)

遗址平面布局示意图
Schematic map of the layout of the site

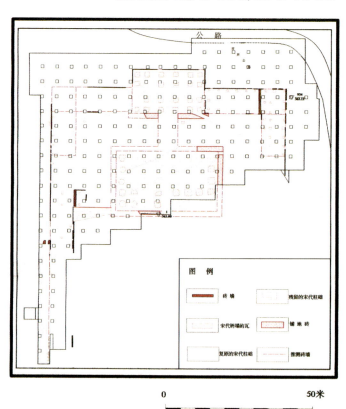

180厘米。F20位于F15的南面，二者相距10.8米。长33.6、宽20.6米。F20与F15的建筑方式相似。但F20规模更大、规格更高。

　　廊庑类建筑均在大殿建筑的两翼，对称分布，建筑面积56～165平方米不等。用条砖砌墙基，有方形或圆形柱坑，坑内置青石为柱础。立柱随建筑单元的开间大小而多寡不一，从6柱到18柱不等。

　　排水设施存在两种类型。一种为外围排水沟，口大底小。沟内普遍填满砖瓦、陶瓷碎片，结构松散。第二种为地下排水管，以两片筒瓦相扣形成，主要设置于低阶地段，用来导出建筑内区的积水。

　　文化遗物可分为两大类，即建筑陶瓷和祭祀陶瓷。其中绝大多数是建筑陶瓷，器类有筒瓦、板瓦、螭吻、鸱尾、滴水、条砖、铺地方砖等。早期的形大质精，器表施透明釉或有青黑色陶衣；晚期的则相反，而且火候特高，有裂胎现象。

祭祀陶瓷大多出土于炭末堆积内,皆为碎片。以碗、盏、杯、碟居多,壶、瓶类较少。其间早期多是釉色晶莹、胎质细腻的薄胎青瓷,作风上承晚唐、五代,铭文、徽记多见于外底。稍后釉色渐杂,胎质渐粗,酱釉瓷成为主流,常见"太"字铭文,往往见于内底。建筑陶瓷和祭祀陶瓷的变化反映出该建筑遗址由盛到衰的发展历程。

建筑陶瓷中,瓦当出土约200件,其中完整或近乎完整的有100余件。分为两大系列,即"王"字兽面纹瓦当与花卉纹瓦当。从功用看,前者与筒瓦配套,用于主体建筑;后者则与短身板瓦配套,用于装饰从属建筑。瓦当与瓦体或通过泥钉对铆,或以平口套合。

在该建筑基址出土的文物中,"如鱼"铭文瓷碗据文献记载具有祭器功用。此外还发现了刻有"歙州斋遗匠人吴四"铭文的筒瓦,从"歙州"地名和筒瓦的形制来看,该建筑的相对年代为北宋。据《宋史》、《太平寰宇记》记载,宋太祖乾德、开宝年间曾先后两次敕修九疑山舜帝陵庙,刻有"开宝……"以及"……作头永清"铭文的残陶片与史实相吻合。因此,该建筑遗迹可能是北宋时期的舜帝陵庙。

玉琯岩宋代建筑遗址布局严谨,规模宏大,是我国唯一一处同时拥有传世文献、存世碑刻、出土古地图和考古发掘资料的舜帝陵庙。在发掘区下部堆积中发现了汉代祭祀坑,和不晚于东汉早期的大型建筑遗迹。所以我们认为,玉琯岩舜帝陵庙的建庙年代可能更早。

大殿建筑遗迹(F20)局部(自北向南摄)
Part of the remains of Pavilion F20 (photo from north to south)

发掘与测绘
Excavation and survey

The Yuguanyan site is situated in a mountain valley 34 km southeast of the seat of Ningyuan County and occupies an area of about 32,000 sq m. In December 2003 to October 2004, the Hunan Provincial Institute of Cultural Relics and Archaeology carried out here a scientific excavation. They obtained important results in the excavated area of 5,000 sq m.

As shown in the extensive area so far revealed, the best preserved are the ruined pavilions of the Song period. Among them the Northern Song remains include the foundations of pavilions and corridors with vestiges of roads and drains. These buildings exhibit the architectural style typical of the Tang-Song period. Meticulous in layout and splendid in scale, they were absolutely not vernacular dwellings, governmental offices and religious temples. The great number, exquisite workmanship and definite uses of the unearthed structural members (animal mask or floral design tile-ends, ridge ornaments, drip-tiles, cylindrical and flat tiles, long narrow bricks and design-decorated square bricks for pavement) all reflect a high construction rank.

It is still more expressive of their nature that some ceramics from the site bear inscriptions "Kai Bao 开宝......," "Shezhou-zhai Qian Jiangren Wu Si (Min) 歙州斋遣匠人吴四 (皿)," "Yi Bei Wu 诣杯吴," "Ru Yu 如鱼," etc. These words are clearly corresponding with the historical records on the events that the first Song emperor ordered twice to repair the legendary emperor Shun memorial temple on Mt. Jiuyi. Therefore, the pavilion complex represented by F15 and F20 may have been the Shun memorial temple built in the Song period.

The Yuguanyan site is the early Shun temple remains unmatchable among their counterparts in the remoteness of literal evidence and in their identification by using simultaneously historical records, handed-down stele-inscriptions, and unearthed ancient maps and material data from excavated sites. In the present excavation area, explorers discovered, in the upper deposits, three phases of building foundation-ditches that arc earlier than Southern Song building layers and, in the lower deposits, sacrificial pits of the Han period and large-sized building remains no later than the Easter Han. Thus it can be believed that the Shun memorial building complex at Yuguanyan was not only built in an early period, but also left over a piece of evidence that sacrificial ceremonies to Emperor Shun were held in succession during the above 1,000 years from the Western Han. Therefore the site of the Song period Yuguanyan memorial building complex to the legendary emperor Shun has incomparable value among its counterparts throughout the whole country. It is of great importance to studying comprehensively the evolution of the sacrificial institution at memorial buildings in ancient China, as well as to researching into the tradition of worshiping Shun and sacrificing to him starting from the Han period.

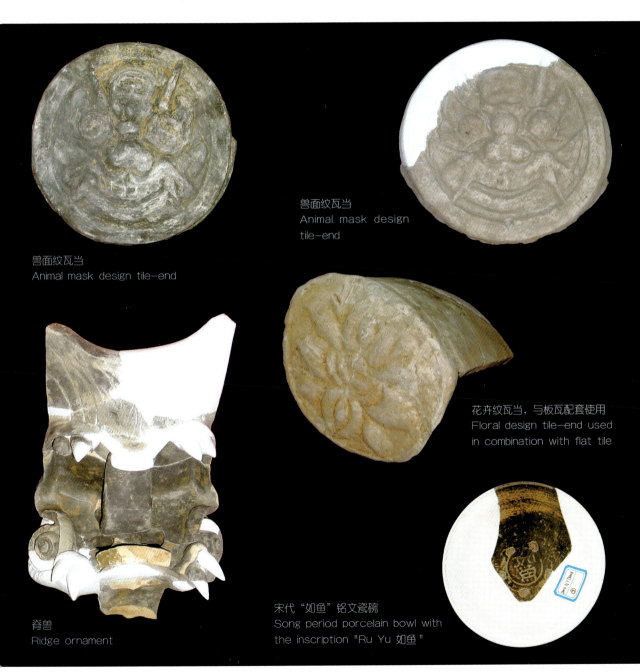

兽面纹瓦当
Animal mask design tile-end

兽面纹瓦当
Animal mask design tile-end

花卉纹瓦当，与板瓦配套使用
Floral design tile-end used in combination with flat tile

脊兽
Ridge ornament

宋代"如鱼"铭文瓷碗
Song period porcelain bowl with the inscription "Ru Yu 如鱼"

杭州南宋临安城
皇城考古新收获

*NEW ACHIEVEMENTS IN THE ARCHAEOLOGICAL
EXPLORATION OF THE IMPERIAL CITY
OF SOUTHERN SONG LIN'AN CITY IN HANGZHOU*

南宋临安城是全国重点文物保护单位。南宋王朝于绍兴八年（1138年）正式以杭州为都城。据史书记载，南宋临安城的皇城位于今杭州市西南的凤凰山东麓，在整个南宋京城的南部。德祐二年（1276年）元兵占领临安，南宋灭亡。此后，元朝有计划地拆毁了南宋皇宫。关于临安城皇城的具体范围以及城内宫殿、宫门、道路等情况，均缺乏详细的文献记载。

1983年，中国社会科学院考古研究所、浙江省文物考古研究所、杭州市文化局组成临安城考古队，定期有计划地进行考古工作，先后找到临安城皇城的东墙和北墙东段。2004年4~8月，为配合临安城皇城总体保护规划，临安城考古队全面展开对皇城的考古勘探调查。最终发现了皇城的北墙西段、南墙和西墙，以及城墙外侧的城壕遗迹，并进一步确认了宫殿中心区域的具体位置。临安城皇城四周范围的确定，为皇城遗址的保护、利用提供了科学依据。

临安城皇城北墙残长约710米。其东端发现于

万松岭路南，至今地面上还残存有部分墙体。自东端向西，皇城北墙开始修建在山坡和山脊上。沿着自然山脉走向，其西端已经呈东北—西南走向。皇城北墙城墙以夹杂石块的黄褐色土和浅灰褐色夯土为主，宽约11米。夯土距地表0.2~0.8、厚0.7~2.7米，夯层厚10~24厘米，皇城墙包括初建和修建两部分，其内侧都有包砌石块的现象。初建夯土城墙的内侧包砌石块3~5层，包石残高0.62、宽0.44米；修建城墙内侧包砌的石块仅残存一层，包石边宽0.4米。

皇城东墙残长约390、宽8.8~12米，位于馒头山东麓，其南段地处馒头山路西侧的断崖上。夯土城墙残宽8.8米，城墙内外两侧可能遭到一些破坏。皇城东墙由黄褐色、浅棕黄色、浅灰褐色夯土构成，距地表深0.4~1.2、厚0.55~1.7米。夯层厚15~30厘米，每层夯土中均夹有砖瓦碎片。

皇城南墙位于今宋城路北侧，大部分与宋城路平行，残长约600米。城墙宽9~14、厚0.5~2米。夯土多为黄褐色，夹杂有小砾石块和少量砖瓦片。

南宋临安城皇城范围示意图
Schematic map of the limits
of the imperial city, Southern
Song Lin'an City

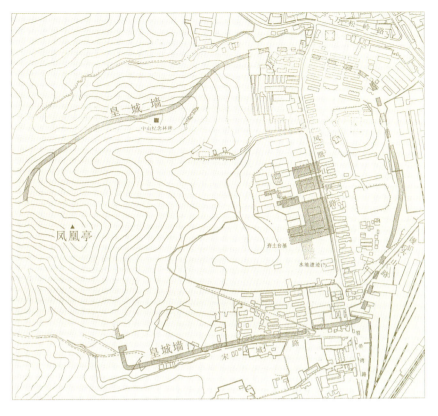

从凤凰亭眺望西湖美景
West Lake's beauty, a distant view from the Fenghuang Pavilion

皇城西墙残长约100、宽约10～11米。西墙南端与南墙衔接，皇城西南角接近直角，西墙向北抵达凤凰山南麓的陡坡，在此没有发现向任何方向延伸的迹象。因此我们初步认为，皇城西墙终止于凤凰山南麓陡坡。在皇城西墙上，还发现一个宽约18米的缺口，缺口两侧的夯土宽20余米。

该缺口可能与皇城西门有关。西墙宽10.5米，距地表深0.12～0.19、残高1.79～1.84米。由黄褐色、浅褐色、浅灰褐夯土构成，密度较大。夯层厚6～20厘米，内含砖瓦残块、瓷片、铜钱等遗物。西墙内侧残存城墙包砖，内侧地面铺有整齐的条砖，条砖下为纯净黄土和砂性生土。皇城西墙并

皇城北墙西段残留的夯土
Rammed-earth left over from the western section of northern wall of the imperial city

皇城南墙位置(今宋城路北侧)
Location of the southern wall of the imperial city (on the northern side of present-day Songcheng Road)

皇城北墙西段及其墙内包砌的石块
Western section of northern wall of the imperial city
and stones in it

皇城西墙内侧包砖
Brick covering on the inner side of the western wall
of the imperial city

不闭合，而是利用了比较陡峻的凤凰山八幡岭之自然山势，与北墙西端形成合围的形式。这在文献中也可得到佐证。

在皇城的南墙、西墙外侧，还勘探出具备城壕功能的排水沟。水沟距离宫城墙12米左右，宽15～20米，距离地表1～1.5米，沟深超过4.5米。此外，在凤凰山脚还发现大型夯土台基5处、水池遗迹3处。

临安城皇城的考古收获主要有以下三个方面。首先是确定了皇城四至范围。皇城东墙位于馒头山东麓；南墙地处宋城路北侧一线，墙外有护城壕；西墙仅建造了南段，而由凤凰山的自然山体替代了大部分皇城西墙；北墙位于万松岭路以南和凤凰山北侧余脉的山脊之上。其次，确认了皇城中心宫殿区，并初步了解到宫殿区的遗迹内涵、保存状况、地层堆积等。收获之三，是历年来在皇城中发掘、采集了大量出土遗物，这为研究临安城的年代和沿革提供了第一手资料。

Based on the results of previous long work, the archaeological researches on the imperial city of Southern Song Li'an City in Zhejiang Hangzhou made a breakthrough in 2004. Archaeological survey, prospecting and trial excavation clarified on the whole the limits of the imperial city in Lin'an, and thus provided a scientific base for the protection and utilization of the imperial city-site.

From April to August 2004, in concert with the planning of the preservation of the imperial city in Lin'an City, the Lin'an City Archaeological Team carried out an extensive survey and prospecting. As a result, they discovered the western section of northern wall and the southern and western walls of the imperial city, brought to light remains of the moat on the outer side of the city-walls, and clarified the exact location of the central palace-area. The imperial city-site measures about 710 m in remaining length for the northern wall, some 390 m for the eastern wall, 600 m or so for the southern

白瓷碗残片
Shard of a white porcelain bowl

青瓷碗残片
Shard of a celadon bowl

青瓷碗残片
Shard of a celadon bowl

绿琉璃器具残片
Broken green-glazed implement

wall, approximately 100 m for the western wall, and roughly 10—11 m in remaining width. The southern end of western wall joins up with the southern wall nearly at a right angle. The northern end of western wall is linked up with the western end of northern wall by the steep Bafan Peak of Mt. Fenghuang, which is also recorded in historical texts.

Outside the southern and western walls, prospectors revealed a 15—20 m wide drain-channel simultaneously functioning as a section of moat. In addition, five large-sized rammed-earth platform-foundations and remains of three water ponds were uncovered on the western side of the road at the foot of Mt. Fenghuang. This locus must have been the central palace-area.

The results of the present archaeological work in the imperial city-site can be summed up as follow: Firstly, the exploration clarified the limits of the imperial city and especially the location its southern and western walls that has puzzled academic circles for a long time. The eastern and western sides of the city are about 800 m apart as the crow flies, while the northern and southern sides, some 600 m. Secondly, the work confirmed the central palace-area of the imperial city and preliminarily uncovered its remaining contents, preservation conditions and strategraphic deposits. Thirdly, the plenty of unearthed objects, along with the previous finds, provided first-hand material for investigating the date and evolution of Lin'an City.

南京建中村南宋墓

THE SOUTHERN SONG TOMB AT JIANZHONG VILLAGE, NANJING

2004年1月中旬，在南京市南郊江宁区江宁镇建中村发现一座大型砖石结构古墓。同年1～2月，南京市博物馆联合江宁区博物馆，对墓葬进行了抢救性发掘。

该墓由封土、墓坑和墓室构成。发掘前，墓上封土大部分已遭施工机械掘毁。在封土中发现一件长方形石质建筑构件。墓坑长方形，方向150°，为砖石结构。坑壁规整，稍微内倾，坑内填土坚硬。墓葬由并列的南、北两个长方形墓室构成，没有发现墓道和墓门。墓室总宽7.94米。北侧墓室略大，全长6.58米；南侧墓室稍小，全长4.82米。两个墓室的结构大体相同，墓壁均由三重砖石构成，厚逾1米，由内到外依次为石灰砖、条石、条砖。墓壁外还用三合土浇浆密封。北侧墓室内的石灰砖外再粉刷一层石灰，使墓壁更加光洁。南侧墓室内，两壁上下各钉入2个铁环。墓顶均用长方形条石封盖，接缝处用铁锤卡合。墓顶外还铺筑厚约20厘米的石灰层。

北侧墓室历史上曾多次遭到盗掘，墓顶局部塌陷，墓室内壁还见有盗墓者留下的凿痕。墓底中部用长方形青砖平铺，四周为制作规整的长方形石板铺地，部分墓砖上模印"大宋绍兴二十五年四月八日……"等多种铭文。墓内满积扰土，只在扰土中发现少量兽骨和晚期陶器碎片。

南侧墓室的砌筑要晚于北侧墓室，没有发现任何盗扰痕迹。其结构相对简陋一些，墓底全

南侧墓室墓顶
Top of the southern tomb-room

墓葬全景
A full view of the tomb

部用长方形青砖错缝平铺一层。墓室中部放置棺椁各一具，木椁盖板部分朽散，余大体完好。木棺外髹黑漆，内存半棺的透明棺液。墓主骨架保存较好，甚至连头发、指甲和少量衣物还未完全腐烂，骨架经初步鉴定为一老年女性。除一件铁质买地券发现于椁底外，其他所有文物皆出自棺内。

棺内出土文物约800件，按质地分为瓷、银、铜、漆木、牙角、玉器以及玻璃、水晶、玛瑙、琥珀等。一些小件佩饰上还遗存有串联的丝线。出土的瓷器有2件定窑白瓷碗，银器主要是罐、盒、箸、

镶宝石银戒指等，铜器有鎏金铜锉、镜、铜钱等。其他还有木质冥钱、木牌饰、木质册书、漆盒、漆葫芦、漆环、牙角质梳、镶银扣牙角质盖盒、竹节形器，以及玻璃盖杯、玻璃龟形饰件、水晶璧、水晶剑格、水晶簪、玛瑙璧、玛瑙人形饰件、各种颜色的料珠等。

出土的玉器数量多，器类丰富，主要有梳、璧、螭龙纹心形佩、簪、印章以及大量的人形、动物形状的玉佩饰。其中动物形玉饰件有鱼、兔、鸡、鸭、鹅、猴、龙头、虎、羊、象等，此外还有辟邪、瓜果、莲、瓶、金刚杵、人、飞天等玉饰件。这些玉

白釉瓷碗
White-glazed porcelain bowl

牙角质香料盒
Ivory and antler perfume-box

玛瑙璧
Agate *bi* disc

玻璃杯
Glass cup

玉梳
Jade comb

饰均出自墓主胸前，其上都有细小穿孔，原应为一套完整的组佩。玉器大多质地温润，雕琢精致，使用了线刻、浮雕、透雕、圆雕、俏色等多种技法，反映出宋代高超的制玉工艺。

其他重要文物还有木钱、木质册书、木牌饰以及满盛香料的牙角质盖盒等。木钱上刻"大德必寿"4字。木质册书2件，可以开合，内夹纸质封册，其上墨书文字多已模糊难辨。木牌饰2件，顶端都有穿孔，两面刻有相同的文字。其中一件呈钟形，上刻"惩忿"2字；另一件呈长方形，上刻"圣功神明非贤莫知固穷轻命审察其机"16字。前者可能用于自勉，而后者可能来自御赐。

据《景定建康志》、《至正金陵新志》等方志记载，墓地近旁的牧龙镇地区是南宋奸相秦桧的家族墓地。20世纪80年代，文物部门曾在附近发掘了秦桧之孙秦埙或秦堪之墓。这次发掘的南宋墓规模大、等级高，出土文物丰富精美，墓室结构独特牢固，墓主可能与秦桧家族有关。

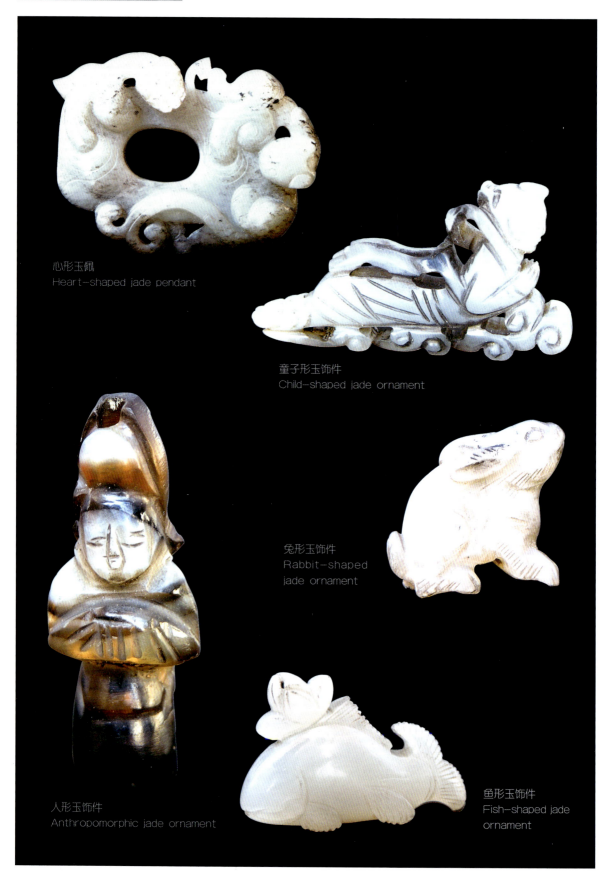

心形玉佩
Heart-shaped jade pendant

童子形玉饰件
Child-shaped jade ornament

兔形玉饰件
Rabbit-shaped
jade ornament

人形玉饰件
Anthropomorphic jade ornament

鱼形玉饰件
Fish-shaped jade
ornament

虎形玉饰件
Tiger-shaped jade ornament

瑞兽形玉饰件
Auspicious-animal-shaped
jade ornament

This tomb lies at Zhaiqian Natural Village of Jianzhong Administrative Village in Jiangning Town of Jiangning District within the southern suburb of Nanjing City. From 29 January to 13 February 2004, in concert with capital construction, the Nanjing Municipal Museum and the Jiangning District Museum carried out a rescuing excavation to explore the grave. The tomb consists of two rectangular rooms arranged side by side from north to south, which measure 6.58 and 4.82 m in length for the northern and southern rooms respectively and 7.94 m in width for either. The tomb-walls are built of bricks and stones in three circles structured of, from the inner to the outer, lime bricks, long narrow stones, and livid bricks. The tomb top is built of rectangular stones for the outer layer (with the joints tightened with iron fasteners) and lime bricks in several courses for the inner layer. The northern room was repeatedly robbed in early days, while the southern one remains intact. The latter is furnished with a chamber and a coffin. The human skeleton from the coffin has been identified as an old woman's remains.

The cultural relics unearthed from the tomb are artifacts in porcelain, silver, bronze, lacquer and wood, jade, glass, crystal, agate, amber, etc., totaling about 800 pieces. They fall into the types of jade comb, *bi* disc and seal, agate *bi*, glass cup, crystal *bi*, silver jar, jeweled silver finger-ring, ivory and antler perfume-box, wooden slips with a list of grave good, wooden plaque, bronze mirror, and anthropomorphic and zoomorphic jade pendant. The jades are not only great in number and rich in variety, but also fine in shape and exquisite in craftsmanship. They considerably enriched the material data of jade working in the Song period. In addition, there are some dozen of glass, crystal, agate and amber articles. Glittering and translucent, they form a batch of rare treasures from the Song period and have high historical and artistic value.

Near the graveyard, a tomb was excavated in the 1980s and has been identified as the burial of Qin Hui's grandson Qin Xun or Qin Kan. The brick epitaph from the memorial temple at that tomb is extremely similar to the one from the Song tomb at Jianzhong. This evidence and local documents suggest that the owner of the present tomb was very likely related to the family of Qin Hui, the notorious treacherous prime minister of the Southern Song Dynasty. The Jianzhong tomb is so far the largest in scale, most complex and solid in structure and richest in grave goods among the Song burials discovered in the Jiangsu region. Its excavation has very great academic value to researching into the tomb-building institute and burial custom of the Song period, as well as to analyzing Qin Hui.

南京明代宝船厂造船遗址

DOCK-SITE OF THE MING PERIOD GOVERNMENTAL SHIPYARD IN NANJING

宝船厂遗址位于南京市西北部的中保村，紧临长江，是目前国内保存面积最大的古代造船遗址。根据《明史》等文献记载，船厂创建于明朝永乐初期，是专为郑和下西洋出访各国所兴建的大型官办造船基地。到20世纪70年代末期，当地尚余7条造船用的船坞，依次被称为一作塘至七作塘。其后由于各种原因，有4条作塘陆续遭到填埋，只有四、五、六3条作塘得以基本保存。3条作塘由北向南平行排列，方向均为北偏东62°。

为迎接郑和下西洋600周年的到来，2003年8月～2004年7月，南京市博物馆考古部对遗址中的六作塘进行了抢救性考古发掘。发掘面积19200平方米，在塘底清理出大量的造船设施，并出土各类文物1500余件。六作塘现存长421、宽约41米。发掘之前，塘内覆盖着厚达3.5米的淤泥。考古队员首先用水枪冲淤，用吸浆泵抽送泥浆，然后按照考

六作塘遗址全景
A full view of the 6th dock-site

9号遗迹的"地钉"结构
Structure of the "ground nails " in the remaining structure No. 9

3号遗迹
Remaining structure No. 3

21 与 22 号遗迹
Remaining structures Nos. 21 and 22

古工作规程进行发掘。

　　清理出的 34 处造船基础设施均坐落于塘底中心线上，除一处外，皆与两侧堤岸垂直。根据构造的不同，我们将其分为三种类型。第一类遗迹数量最多，是由竖立的木桩围成一圈，大部分围成长方形，少数围成椭圆形或 8 字形。在大多数的木桩圈内，塘底生土之上铺设厚达 20～40 厘米的红色或绿色的砂石土层。有的则利用较长的木料，一排排横铺于地表之上。其作用都是为了在塘底创造出较为坚实、干燥的工作面，以利于其上的造船施工。

　　第二类以 3 号遗迹为代表，这是一处用大木头层层叠架、多达 4 层的造船遗迹。它的最底层是密集的底桩，用直径 8～15 厘米的木桩笔直地打入生土，约 1.1 米深。其上铺设厚约 30 厘米的绿色土，在绿色土层之上铺设大木。

　　第三类遗迹是榫卯框架结构。以 24 号遗迹为

例，它南北长 10.7、东西宽 3.9 米，框架平面呈"日"字形。框架所用木料都经过加工，光滑规整。在榫卯框架内侧，竖立一圈木桩，紧贴着边框，围成长方形。两者之间还插有一层竹席。该遗迹底部也有密集的底桩，排列方式为一排竖桩间隔一排横桩。

　　通过对地层的分析我们认为，宝船厂遗址原来是长江岸边的河漫滩，明代修建船厂时，先在作塘的位置挖淤加深，形成塘口。塘中挖出的淤土就近堆积在两边。同时从它处运来黄土，在两侧堆积、加高，经过夯打形成堤岸，但未修建砖石护堤。

　　已获取的千余件文物绝大部分出土于塘内，从质地上看，有木、铁、棕、石、陶瓷器等。按其用途可以分成三类。第一类是船用构件，其中数量最多的是各种形状的船板。许多船板凿有方形或圆形的钉孔。有的船板上带有精美的雕花装饰，或者残存红、蓝、黑色的油漆。个别船板上刻有文字，标

明其在船上的安装位置。此类文物
中，最重要的发现是两根保存完好
的舵杆，均为方头扁尾，长度分别
是 10.1 和 11 米。头部带有 2 个长
方形穿孔，用来安装舵；尾部刻有
3 个长方形浅槽，用来安装舵叶。在
塘中还出土了近百枚打制而成的石
球，直径从 6 厘米至 12 厘米不等，
其用途可能是炮弹之类的武器，也
可能是船上的压舱石。

　　第二类是造船时使用的各种
工具和用具。如铁制的斧、凿、锯、
锉、钻、锥、刀，以及各式铁钉。此
外还有木制的锤、桨、夯、刮刀、T
形撑，以及用来填补船缝的油泥

榫卯结构
Tenon-and-mortise structure

7号遗迹
Remaining structure No. 7

1号舵杆在塘中的情况
Rudder No. 1 on the dock-site

2号舵杆出土情况
Rudder No. 2 being
excavated from the
dock-site

坨。在塘底出土了一根木尺，长31.1厘米，背后还刻有"魏家琴记"铭文。塘内出土了大量的碗、盏、杯、碟等瓷器，不少器底有带有姓氏的墨书痕迹，应为当时造船工人所使用的日常器皿。

第三类是造船设施构件，主要是各种木桩、木柱和木板，它们大都是从造船遗迹上散落下来的。在不少木桩、木柱上发现有铭文，铭文的制作包括刀刻、烙烧、墨书等多种方法，其内容多为数字编号和尺寸。另外在塘中还出土了水车龙骨残件，这是当时筑坝抽水、放船进出船坞时必须使用的设备。

船坞遗址是国内外考古实践中的"冷门"，可资借鉴的先例极少。对宝船厂六作塘遗址的发掘，为今后开展类似的考古工作积累了经验。

铁质工具
Iron tools

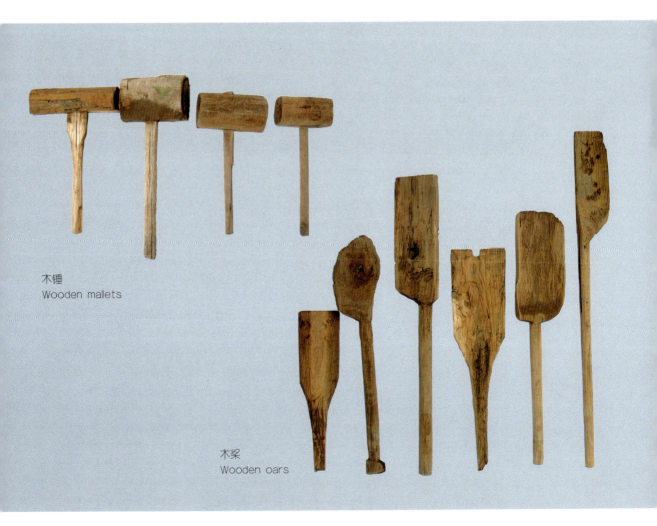

木锤
Wooden mallets

木桨
Wooden oars

石球
Stone balls

This shipyard site is situated in the northwest of Nanjing City, to the east of the Yangtze River. It was built in the early Ming period and functioned as a large shipbuilding base under the control of the Ming government. A lot of ships used in Zheng He's seven expeditions to the Western world were built at this dockyard. As late as the 1970s, there still remained seven shipbuilding docks, which were called first to seventh docks. Later, owing to different causes, four docks were successively buried, only the fourth to sixth ones continued existing for a period.

To greet the 600th anniversary of Zheng He's expeditions that will come in 2005, the Archaeological Department of Nanjing Municipal Museum carried out a rescuing excavation on the sixth dock-site from August 2003 to August 2004. They excavated an area of 19,200 sq m, revealed 34 remaining structures, and brought to light more than 1,500 cultural relics.

The site of the governmental shipyard was originally a stretch of flood land on the bank of Yangtze River in the Ming period. To built the shipyard, hollows were dug here and embankments on their two sides were formed by piling up and ramming the loess fetched from nearby areas. The sixth dock-site is 421 m long and some 41 m wide. As known from excavation, this was a well-planned and elaborately built busy shipbuilding workshop.

The revealed 34 remaining structures are all along the central axis of the dock bottom. They can be roughly divided into three types. The first type is a sort of enclosure formed of stakes, generally rectangular and occasionally oval or "8"-shaped. The second is made of crisscross logs by piling them layer on layer. The third is formed of logs that are jointed with tenons and mortises. In the bottom of these structures are densely-disposed base stakes, the so-called "ground nails" recorded in the *Yingzao Fashi* (《营造法式》 *Building Standards*).

The cultural relics are largely yielded from inside the dock-site. They fall into three categories in terms of use.

The first category consists of structural members of ships. Most of them are ship decks varying in shape. But the most important finds are two intact rudders, which are 10.1 and 11 m long respectively and roughly the same in shape, either having a square head and a flat tail.

The second category embraces various shipbuilding tools and implements. These include iron axes, chisels, saws, files, drills, awls, knives and nails, as well as wooden mallets, oars, rams, scrapers and "T"-shaped supports.

In the third category are structural members of shipbuilding equipment. They were scattered from vestiges of various structures. Among them are wood stakes, posts and boards, and also a broken water wheel, maybe left over from a water draining installation used in the construction of embankments.